Contents

Acknowledgments
Introduction
1. What Is Domestic Violence and Abuse?
2. Who Abuses Whom?
3. Types of Abuse
4. Increased Risk of Death
5. How Domestic Violence Starts
6. Perpetrators of Domestic Violence
7. The Domestic Violence Cycle
8. Victims of Abuse
9. How Domestic Violence Affects Children
10. Signs of Domestic Violence and What to Do
11. Leaving an Abusive Relationship
12. Myths and Realities of Domestic Violence
13. How the Law Views Domestic Violence/Getting a Restraining Order
14. Useful Terminology in Understanding Domestic Violence
15. Domestic Violence Statistics
16. How and Where to Get Help Now
Resources
References
About the Author
About Dr. Bray

Acknowledgments

The information contained in this guide is not unique, nor could it be; it draws on the accumulated efforts, research, and results of professionals who work with victims of domestic violence.

I am especially grateful to those with whom I work who strive to understand the behaviors and nuances of people who are affected by domestic violence—the perpetrators, victims and the children. This guide attempts to touch on many aspects of abuse with the intention that it may lead the reader to explore the subject further within the context of their own experiences.

This guide is just that—a guide. It is written to provide the reader with an overview of the definition and dynamics of domestic violence and abuse. While most recorded abuse is male on female violence, research is showing high rates of female on male violence and within the LGBTQ$^+$ community. A key word to look out for in reviewing statistics is the word "reported." Most episodes of abuse go unreported.

As you read please replace the gender in the definitions to fit your own experience of abuse. Use the guide as a means of deciding what to do next to help yourself. It can also be used as a stepping-off point to learn more about any specific area in which you have an interest.

Domestic violence is a common behavior experienced across every culture, gender relationship, and social and demographic strata. If you think that you are a victim of domestic violence please know that you are not alone. There is help available—just a phone call away—from people who understand what you are going through and who can help you if you reach out to them.

Each experience of domestic violence is unique. That said you will be surprised how much victims (and perpetrators) of abuse have in common and how much those who help victims have to offer to help.

Nobody deserves to experience domestic violence or abuse of any kind. Not you. Not anybody else. Please reach out and talk to someone who can help you.

I am very grateful to all of the people with whom I have worked as a Guardian ad Litem in Dependency, Domestic Violence and Family Courts in Palm Beach and Miami, Florida since 2005.

I am especially grateful to the victims, and their families, of domestic violence with whom I have worked for sharing their stories and their lives with me through the difficult times they experienced.

Judge Carroll Kelly for her resilience and expertise in the work that she does in Domestic Violence Court. Judge Cindy Lederman (retired) for her lifelong advocacy for the children—and families—in her care in Miami, Florida.

To my friend Alan Abramowitz, the Executive Director of the Statewide Guardian ad Litem Program in Florida. Susan Somers Esq, supervising attorney Guardian ad Litem Program in Miami. The domestic violence case managers in Miami, and the domestic violence attorneys who provide tireless representation for the victims of domestic violence whom they represent. My friend Ken Lanning, Special Agent FBI (retired) for the wisdom and specialist knowledge in human behavior that he has imparted to me personally and through his many publications. My friend Celia Quintas, Ph.D., family therapist, with whom I have worked for many years for the extensive and meaningful work that she has done with the children and victims of domestic violence who have been referred to her therapeutic care.

My thanks to my longtime friends Morgan Soumah and Elizabeth Eason for their dedication to helping and protecting victims of domestic abuse and child abuse.

Finally, a word of thanks to my wife, Laura Daly, a Director at Jackson Memorial Hospital, Miami, who, when I asked her what I could do to be of service to others, suggested that I become a Guardian ad Litem. And I did.

Introduction

Not every perpetrator of domestic violence is violent. Not every act of domestic violence is violent in the way that we understand the term "violent."

There are several terms to describe domestic violence, for example, family violence, intimate partner violence (IPV), battering, domestic abuse, sexual abuse and others. The term "domestic violence" is used as an umbrella term to cover them all. **The term "domestic violence" is used throughout this guide to describe violent and non-violent abuse.**

Domestic "violence" can seem like an exclusionary term for some victims as their abuser has never hit them or threatened to do so. The two words "domestic violence" describe a wide group of behaviors including physical and sexual violence, emotional abuse, psychological abuse, financial abuse, neglect, threats of violence and others. Domestic violence describes a pattern of repeated behavior, although it can be a one-off event as well.

Abusers have many different styles of abuse. Abuse is all about power and control. Some abusers are more intense in their abuse than others. Abuse may be blatant, or subtle. Some abusers are predictable in their behaviors while others are not. Each experience of domestic violence is unique to the victim. Some perpetrators abuse constantly; others occasionally. Abuse can also be interlaced with times of kindness.

Abusers may follow a predictable cycle of tension, abuse, and reconciliation as are described later in this guide. Others don't; they abuse as they see fit. **It's not about anger. Research shows that most partner-abusive men do not present with anger-related disturbances.**[1] It's about an *attitude*.

Not all perpetrators of abuse are the same. Not all domestic violence is the same. What is the same is the attitude of the perpetrator.

Abuse grows from attitudes and values, not feelings. The roots are ownership, the trunk is entitlement and the branches are control. Abusers are unwilling to be non-abusive, not unable. They do not want to give up power and control.[2]

Early warning signs of abuse may include:

- They are disrespectful about their former partners
- They are disrespectful towards you
- They do favors for you that you don't want or put on such a show of generosity that it makes you uncomfortable
- They are controlling
- They are possessive
- Nothing is ever their fault
- They are self-centered
- They may abuse alcohol or drugs
- They pressure you for sex
- They may be physically abusive or threaten you
- They get serious too quickly about the relationship
- They intimidate you when they are angry, threatening you with violence
- They have double standards. What's not allowed for you is fine for them.
- They have negative attitudes toward women and/or men
- They treat you differently around other people
- They appear to be attracted to vulnerability[3]

Note to Reader

The terms "abuser," "perpetrator," and "offender" are used interchangeably throughout this guide.

The use of "he" and "she" pronouns are the default means of referring to domestic violence perpetrators and victims. They may also be he/he, she/she, she/he or they/them. Please use whatever combination reflects your experience.

1. What Is Domestic Violence and Abuse?

> "Domestic violence is not rare. It occurs at all levels of the American society, and all classes of community, regardless of social, economic, or cultural backgrounds."
> —Judge Bill Swann, Fourth Circuit Court, Sixth Judicial District of Tennessee

WHAT IS DOMESTIC VIOLENCE?

Domestic violence (also called intimate partner violence or IPV, domestic abuse, or relationship abuse) is a pattern of behaviors used by one partner to extert and maintain power and control over another partner in an intimate or dependent relationship.[4]

Domestic violence includes victimizations committed by intimate partners (current or former spouses, boyfriends, or girlfriends), immediate family members (parents, children, or siblings), and other relatives.

Domestic violence is a *pattern* of controlling behaviors—including violence or threats of violence—that one person uses to establish power over an intimate partner in order to control that partner's actions and activities. It may also be a one-time event. Domestic violence is not a disagreement, a marital argument, or an anger management problem. Domestic violence is abusive, disrespectful, and hurtful behaviors that one intimate partner chooses to use against the other partner.

The U.S. Department of Justice defines domestic violence as "A pattern of abusive behavior in any relationship that is used by one partner to gain or maintain power and control over another intimate partner. Domestic violence can be physical, sexual, emotional, economic, or psychological actions or threats of actions that influence another person. This includes any behaviors that intimidate, manipulate, humiliate, isolate, frighten, terrorize, coerce, threaten, blame, hurt, injure, or wound someone."[5]

In 2019 the Department of Justice updated its definition to: "The term 'domestic violence' includes felony or misdemeanor crimes of violence committed by a current or former spouse or intimate partner of the victim, by a person with whom the victim shares a child in common, by a person who is cohabitating with or has cohabitated with the victim as a spouse or intimate partner, by a person similarly situated to a spouse of the victim under the domestic or family violence laws of the jurisdiction receiving grant monies, or by any other person against an adult or youth victim who is protected from that person's acts under the domestic or family violence laws of the jurisdiction."[6]

DEFINITIONS OF DOMESTIC VIOLENCE (DV), INTIMATE PARTNER VIOLENCE (IPV), AND DOMESTIC ABUSE (DA)

Generally, the terms *domestic violence, intimate partner violence,* and *domestic abuse* are often—incorrectly—used interchangeably. They refer to different behaviors. Specifically, domestic violence (DV), intimate partner violence (IPV) and domestic abuse (DA) refer to three different things:

1. **Domestic violence** refers to violence—assault and battery—perpetrated in the home, against partners, children, and elders. It includes sexual assault. It includes physical damage to property or pets.
2. **Intimate partner violence** refers to violence between intimate partners including LGBTQ⁺ (lesbian, gay, bisexual, transgender, queer or questioning) couples.
3. **Domestic abuse** refers to forms of abuse that are not violent but are just as damaging that include verbal abuse, economic abuse, social isolation, financial control, and emotional and psychological abuse. A person does not have to be hit to be hurt.

The three types may be present on their own or all together in the home.

In this guide, the term *domestic violence* (DV) is used throughout to describe all types of domestic abuse unless otherwise noted, as that is the umbrella term used.

DEFINING AN ABUSIVE INTIMATE RELATIONSHIP

Domestic violence refers to abuse in an intimate relationship.

An intimate relationship is one in which two people, *of any sexual orientation or identity,* are dating, living together, married, or separated. The two people are well-known to each other and have, or have had, emotional ties to each other. In many cases, they will also have economic, family, and other ties.

Who Is an Intimate Partner?

An intimate partner is a person with whom one has a close personal relationship that may be characterized by the following:

- Emotional connections
- Regular contact
- Ongoing physical contact and/or sexual behavior
- Identify as a couple
- Familiarity and knowledge about each other's lives

The relationship need not involve all these dimensions. Examples of intimate partners include current or former spouses, boyfriends or girlfriends, dating partners, or sexual partners. IPV can occur between heterosexual or same-sex couples and does not require sexual intimacy.[7]

Ninety percent of the time the best predictor of domestic violence is past behavior.[8]

You may be experiencing domestic violence if your partner is doing any of these or other unwanted behaviors:

- Hurting you physically: slapping, hair pulling, strangling, hitting, kicking, punching, grabbing, excessively squeezing or shaking, twisting your arms, burning you, or intentionally injuring you in any way.
- Verbally abusing you
- Using your children against you
- Calling you names and hurting you emotionally
- Harming your pets
- Acting with extreme jealousy and possessiveness
- Isolating you from family and friends
- Threatening to commit suicide or to kill you
- Controlling your money

- Withholding medical help
- Abandoning you, especially while pregnant
- Stalking you
- Demanding sex or unwanted sexual practices
- Hiding assistive devices if you have a handicap
- Minimizing the destructive behavior
- Threatening to "out" you if you are LGBTQ⁺
- Controlling you with "that certain look" or gestures [9]

All of the tactics above are abusive, and some may also constitute a crime.

DOMESTIC VIOLENCE IS ABOUT POWER AND CONTROL

Domestic violence is not about losing control or an inability to manage anger. It is about the abuse of power to exert control over another human being.

It is about the abuser choosing to use a variety, and pattern, of abusive behaviors, to gain and maintain control over their partner. It involves not only a behavior, but also the behavior's meaning to the people involved, its intent, and its effect on the victim.[10]

Domestic violence is a pattern of violent and/or coercive behaviors that a person uses against an intimate partner and others in the household in order to gain power and control in that relationship. The behaviors exerted can include physical, sexual, emotional, economic abuse and neglect.

TYPES OF DOMESTIC VIOLENCE PERPETRATORS

Not all abuse is by men toward women. Perpetrators of abuse include:

1. Men who commit violence against women.
2. Women who commit violence against men.
3. Men who commit violence against other men, including in LGBTQ⁺ relationships.
4. Women who commit violence against other women, including

LGBTQ⁺ relationships.
5. Adults who commit violence against children (child abuse and neglect).
6. Adults who commit violence against elders (elder abuse).
7. Adults who commit violence against vulnerable or disabled adults.
8. Adolescents who commit violence against adults, siblings, or children.

Throughout this guide, references to the sex of the abusers, or victims, can be interchanged to suit the reader's experience.

2. Who Abuses Whom?

While most recorded abuse is male on female violence, emerging research is showing high rates of female on male violence and in the LGBTQ⁺ community. A key word to look out for in reviewing statistics on domestic violence is the word "reported." Most episodes of abuse go unreported.[11]

PREVALENCE OF DOMESTIC VIOLENCE/DOMESTIC ABUSE

It is hard to know exactly how common domestic violence is because most people don't report it. An estimated 33 percent—one in three—of intimate relationships or marriages experience domestic violence or abuse.

Domestic violence can happen in any relationship, and even after the relationship has ended. Both men and women can be abusers or abused.[12]

RATE OF DOMESTIC VIOLENCE IN HETEROSEXUAL AND LGBTQ⁺ RELATIONSHIPS

Research into domestic violence began in the 1970s in response to the women's movement. Traditionally studies focused on women abused by men in heterosexual relationships.

Recent studies in the U.S. have shown that the rate of domestic violence among LGBTQ⁺ couples may be the same as for opposite-sex relationships. In 2013, the Centers for Disease Control and Prevention (CDC) released figures showing the high prevalence of domestic violence in same-sex relationships. Another study from Northwestern University shows that the rate of domestic violence may be even higher among LGBTQ⁺ couples.[12,13]

ABUSE AGAINST MEN

Emerging research is showing high rates of domestic abuse and violence where men are the victims. The reason for abuse is the same for men and women—it's about maintaining power and control over a partner. The data on the actual prevalence of domestic violence against men is not available at the same level as it is recording abuse against women.

In 2010, the Centers for Disease Control and Prevention released data from its National Intimate Partner and Sexual Violence Survey. According to the CDC's statistics—estimates based on more than 18,000 telephone-survey responses in the United States—5,365,000 men had been victims of intimate partner physical violence in the previous 12 months, compared with 4,741,000 women. By the study's definition physical violence includes slapping, pushing, and shoving. Approximately 40 percent of the victims of severe physical violence were men. The CDC repeated the survey in 2011, the results of which were published in 2014, and found almost identical numbers—with the percentage of male victims having suffered severe physical violence having risen.

According to the same report, women experience sexual violence and stalking at higher rates than men.[12,14]

Gender roles are an important issue. Society regards women as the nurturers and caregivers; men as the providers and protectors. To consider that a woman may take on the role of an abuser threatens society's gender-role assignment. As a result, many men are told to "suck it up," or face further shaming for identifying the severity of the problem.

Physical violence carried out against men is often similar to physical violence against women though it can differ. In some instances, to make up for the differences in physical strength, women might use weapons including bats, kitchen utensils, guns, or knives.

Women may engage in emotional abuse and psychological abuse; controlling mechanisms that can include humiliation, intimidation, and belittling words or statements. Men may fear that others will think they are lying, or that they are actually the ones perpetrating the abuse.[15,16,17]

Domestic Violence in the Lesbian/Gay/Bisexual/Transgender/Queer, Questioning Community (LGBTQ⁺)

LGBTQ⁺ refers to an individual who identifies as lesbian, gay, bisexual, transgender, queer or questioning.

Research shows that LGBTQ⁺ members fall victim to domestic violence at equal or even higher rates when compared to their heterosexual counterparts. LGBTQ⁺ domestic violence is underreported, unacknowledged, and often reported as something other than domestic violence.[18,19]

Abuse Tactics

LGBTQ⁺ abusive partners use many of the same tactics as heterosexual abusive partners such as social isolation, emotional and psychological abuse, economic control, and physical and sexual violence in order to gain and maintain power and control over their intimate partners. However, domestic violence within same-sex relationships is comprised of some unique characteristics and includes the use of anti-LGBTQ⁺ societal stigma and bias as a tactic to exert power and control and increase isolation.[20]

Issues and Barriers Unique to LGBTQ⁺ Victims of Domestic Violence

There are several aspects of domestic violence that can be unique to the LGBTQ⁺ community. Some of these may act as a barrier against the victim seeking help.

- LGBTQ⁺ abusive partners may "out" (or threaten to "out") their victims, thereby exposing the victims' sexual orientation, gender identity, and/or HIV status to family, employers, police, religious institutions, the community, or child protective workers.
- LGBTQ⁺ abusive partners often control their partners' expressions of sexual identity and connections to, and within, the larger LGBTQ⁺ community.
- LGBTQ⁺ abusive partners may sabotage or disallow a transgendered partner access to his/her prescribed hormones, often medically required during the transition process.
- LGBTQ⁺ abusive partners may use children in common to manipulate and control the victim around issues of custody and visitation, particularly in cases where the child(ren) are biologically related to the abusive partner and may or may not be legally adopted by the victim.
- Service providers and/or first responders often make assumptions about, and perpetuate the myth that same-sex intimate partners cannot perpetuate (or be victims of) domestic violence, as both partners are

assumed to share equal social standing, earning potential, and physical strength, and are therefore unable to exert power and control over, or be controlled by an intimate partner.

- Dual arrests are common within the LGBTQ⁺ community, as the lack of gender disparity often makes primary aggressor determinations more challenging than the statistically established norm of male perpetrator/female victim within heterosexual domestic violence.
- LGBTQ⁺ individuals may be overlooked by mandatory domestic-violence victim notification at hospitals.
- Individuals who have not publicly disclosed their LGBTQ⁺ status, who have that information exposed by an abusive partner, become more visible, putting them at risk for becoming vulnerable targets for general criminal behavior even outside of their intimate relationships.[21]

Transgender Intimate Partner Violence

Transgender individuals may suffer from a greater burden of intimate partner violence than gay or lesbian individuals. Transgender victims of intimate partner violence are more likely to experience threats or intimidation, harassment, and police violence within domestic or intimate partner violence. Specific forms of abuse occur within relationships where one partner is transgender, including:

- Using offensive pronouns such as "it" to refer to the transgender partner
- Mocking the transgender partner's body and/or appearance
- Telling the transgender partner that he or she is not a real man or woman
- Ridiculing the transgender partner's identity as "bisexual," "trans," "femme," "butch," "gender queer," etc.[22]

For statistical information see Chapter 15, Domestic Violence Statistics.

3. Types of Abuse

TYPES OF DOMESTIC VIOLENCE AND ABUSE

Not all abuse involves physical violence. Not all abusers employ all the methods that are listed here. They may use one type or a combination. Their behaviors may escalate. They use whatever they find works to control the victim.

Domestic violence is implemented in a variety of methods:

Physical Assault: the intentional use of physical force with the potential for causing death, disability, injury, or harm. It includes any physical act—pinching, grabbing, throwing, beating, pushing, shoving, slapping, punching, shaking, hitting with objects, stabbing, suffocating, biting, strangling, shooting, burning, killing. It may include the use of a weapon or the use of restraints or the abuser's body, size, weight, or strength against another person.

A threat of violence *is* violence

Sexual Abuse or assault is divided into three categories:

1. Use of physical force to compel a person to engage in a sexual act against his or her will, whether or not the act is completed;
2. Attempted or completed sex act involving a person who is unable to understand the nature or condition of the act, to decline participation, or to communicate unwillingness to engage in the sexual act, e.g., because of illness, disability, or the influence of alcohol or other drugs, or because of intimidation or pressure; and
3. Abusive sexual contact. This includes rape within a relationship.

Other examples include exposure to sexually transmitted diseases, not using contraception, or being forcibly subjected to pornographic or violent sexual material. It includes a male deliberately trying to impregnate a female or a female deliberately trying to get pregnant as a means of controlling their partner. May include sextortion which is blackmail in which sexual information or images of the victim are used to extort sexual favors and/or money from the victim or they are used to damage the victim's reputation.

Emotional Abuse: includes belittling the victim in private or publicly. Also includes systematic verbal humiliation and/or intimidating threats aimed directly at the partner or at what is valuable to the partner—including threat of attacks against property or pets. It may include threats of suicide by the perpetrator, or threats of harm to children or other family members.

Psychological Abuse: intimidation, threatening harm, manipulation/gaslighting, kidnapping, harassment, hurting or killing pets, destruction of property; also use and abuse of children to control the adult victim, poisoning the children's minds against the nonoffending partner, threats of suicide or homicide if she leaves or reports the abusive behaviors.

Neglect/Economic abuse refers to the control of financial resources by the perpetrator in a way that blocks the victim's access to them when needed; include denying access to money or credit cards; refusing to pay bills; denying food, clothing, and/or transportation; depriving them of money to purchase the most basic of items, abandoning the partner, abandoning the partner when pregnant or following giving birth.

Social abuse refers to the isolation of the victim, blocking access to social supports and resources. Possessiveness, jealousy, suspicions of sexual infidelity or emotional disloyalty, and/or extreme demands for the partner's time and attention result in the partner's increasing isolation. **It may include the misuse or modification of religious scripture to explain abusive behavior as allowed or required to satisfy the abuser's wishes.**

Stalking can be a form of psychological abuse and/or include threats of violence. This includes cyberstalking, such as the perpetrator constantly texting or calling the victim, the use of apps to listen in on the victim's phone calls/voicemail or texts, use of apps to track the victim's phone and location, hacking into their social network sites or email to know where they are, what they are doing, and who they are with. It also includes physical stalking of the victim—following them to work, home, school, or on social outings, refusing to let them go on trips for business or pleasure without the abusive partner present.[23,24]

Stalking behaviors include:

- Repeated, unwanted intrusive and frightening communications from the perpetrator by text, phone or email. Repeatedly leaving or sending

victim unwanted items, gifts or flowers.
- Following or waiting for the victim at their home, school, workplace, store, gym or places where they go to enjoy themselves.
- Making direct or indirect threats to harm the victim, the victim's children, relatives, friends or pets. This may include threats to the victim's reputation through social media or other means.
- Damaging or threatening to damage the victim's home, car or property.
- Harassing the victim through social media.
- Posting information or spreading rumors about the victim on social media, in public places or by word of mouth.
- Obtaining personal information about the victim by accessing public records, through the Internet, using private investigators, by going through the victim's trash, following the victim, contacting the victim's friends, family members, work or neighbors.[25]

See "How a Perpetrator Can Track You" on page 86.

Consequential Emotional Abuse

All abuse has one type of abuse in common—consequential emotional abuse. This is the emotional abuse felt as a consequence of being abused.

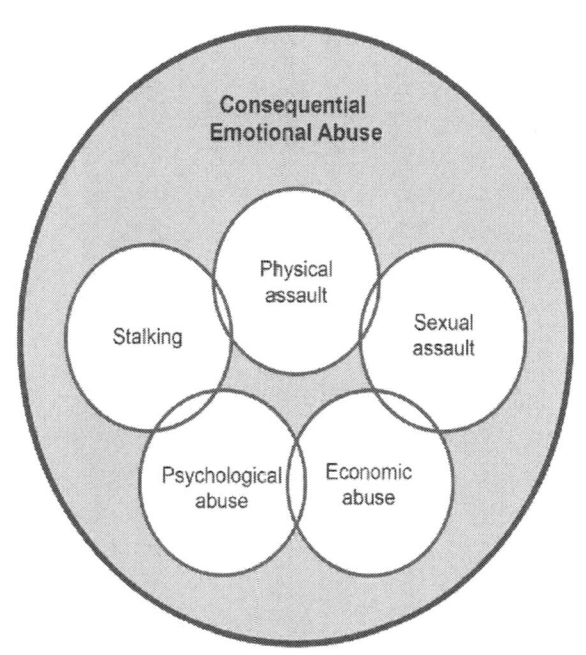

Domestic abuse types rarely occur in isolation.[26]

It is rare for one type of abuse to occur without another

Many of the types of abuse occur concurrently; for example, physical abuse and isolation, rape and neglect, stalking and emotional abuse—any and all combinations are possible.

Domestic violence is rarely a single event (although it can be)—it is usually a pattern of events.

Emotional abuse in domestic violence is the most long-lasting

Victims who have experienced physical, verbal, and emotional abuse state unequivocally that the emotional and verbal abuse is the most hurtful and has the most damaging long-term effects.[27,28]

4. Increased Risk of Death

There are certain factors that increase the risk of death in domestic violence relationships.

The ultimate form of control, or domestic violence, is the threat of death or death itself. Threats of harm desensitize the perpetrator and allow them to mentally rehearse what may become homicide.

1. Access to a firearm: The best indicators of the risk of homicide are threats of death or deadly harm from the perpetrator accompanied by their access to a firearm. Research has repeatedly shown that domestic abusers with guns inflict a disproportionate amount of lethal violence on their spouses and partners. **Abused women are five times more likely to be killed by their abuser if the abuser owns or has access to a firearm.**[29] In the U.S. approximately three women die at the hands of a current or former intimate partner *every day*. Others die in acts of murder-suicide, which is the ultimate demonstration that if the perpetrator can't have the victim, nobody can.[30,31]

In the United States, homicide is a leading cause of death among black and young women (aged 15–24 years), regardless of pregnancy status, and the majority of homicides among all women of reproductive age are carried out with firearms.[32,33]

In domestic violence, the three reasons guns are used frequently is that they are more efficient than other weapons, they can be used impulsively, and they can be used to terrorize and threaten.

In a study of partner homicides, perpetrators who killed with guns were asked if they would have used another weapon if a gun were not available; most said no.

Research demonstrates that those areas with greater restrictions on firearm ownership have lower incidences of domestic violence homicide.[34]

2. Strangulation: Strangulation is defined as "intentionally impeding normal breathing or circulation of the blood by applying pressure on the throat or neck by blocking the nose or mouth of another person."

Victims of one episode of strangulation are seven to eight times more likely to become a homicide victim at the hands of the same partner.

Strangulation is one of the most terrorizing and lethal forms of violence used by men against their female intimate partners. The act of strangulation symbolizes an abuser's power and control over the victim. The sensation of suffocating can be terrifying; the victim is completely overwhelmed by the abuser. A single traumatic experience of strangulation, or the threat of it, may instill such intense fear that the victim can get trapped in a pattern of control by the abuser and made vulnerable to further abuse. Experts across the medical profession now agree that manual or ligature strangulation is "lethal force" and is **one of the best predictors of a future homicide in domestic violence cases**. Strangulation can cause substantial (and often delayed) injuries.

With repeated strangulation attempts the purpose of the abuser is not to kill the victim but to demonstrate that they have the ability to kill them.[35]

3. Leaving the relationship: Leaving the relationship has been shown to be one of the most dangerous times for the victim. **Of the women who are killed by their partners, 75 percent are killed after they have left the abusive relationship.**[36]

4. Pregnancy: Homicide was found to be the second-leading cause of injury-related death for pregnant women, after car accidents, in a study by the National Institutes of Health. The National Coalition Against Domestic Violence (NCADV) found that between 1990 and 2004, 1,300 pregnant women in the U.S. were murdered, with 56 percent being shot to death (the rest were stabbed or strangled). More than two-thirds were killed during their first trimester.[37]

Domestic Violence Homicide and Murder-Suicide

Homicide-followed-by-suicide ("homicide-suicide") incidents are defined as violent acts during which a person kills one or more individuals and then commits suicide. These incidents account for roughly 1,000–1,500 violent deaths annually in the United States, or 20–30 deaths weekly.[37a]

Approximately 75% of homicide-suicide incidents involve a male perpetrator killing a current or former female intimate partner, many homicide-suicide incidents also involve child victims.

Of a study of 408 murder-suicide cases, most perpetrators were men (91 percent) and most used a gun (88 percent). A 12-city study of these cases found that domestic violence had previously occurred in 70 percent of them.

Most people who commit murder-suicide are non-Hispanic white males who kill their mates or former mates. Prior domestic violence is the greatest risk factor in these cases.

Access to a gun is a significant risk factor, as are threats of violence with a weapon, a stepchild in the home, or separation from their partners. Unemployment was a significant risk factor for murder-suicide but only when combined with a history of domestic violence.[38]

Risk of Death from Suicide

Women who experience domestic violence, particularly sexual abuse, are at increased risk for suicidal ideation or behavior than the general population. **In a national study, heterosexual women who had experienced physical violence by a partner were more than seven times more likely to report current suicidal ideation than their counterparts who had not experienced domestic violence**, after allowing for socio-demographic variables, childhood abuse, and psychiatric disorders. Other research suggests that the more severe the domestic violence, the greater the risk for suicidal ideation or attempts by the victim.

Studies have found that domestic violence victims have higher-than-average rates of suicidal thoughts, with as many as 23 percent of survivors having attempted suicide compared to 3 percent among populations with no prior domestic-violence exposure. It's not just physical violence that's linked with an increase in suicide. Verbal and emotional abuse are also connected with higher risk, as well as the duration, frequency and severity of abuse, and the presence of other factors such as post-traumatic stress disorder (PTSD), childhood trauma, depression and substance use.[39,40]

Domestic Violence: Also Deadly for Police

Domestic violence calls are among the most dangerous for police. Police officers are more likely to be killed responding to domestic disputes and disturbances than any other type of call.[41]

5. How Domestic Violence Starts

NOT EVERY CONFLICT IS DOMESTIC VIOLENCE

People in intimate relationships almost inevitably have moments when they are hurtful to each other. Occasional hitting, shoving, name-calling, and "button-pushing" may be experienced in many relationships without inducing generalized fear or physical injury. This does not constitute domestic violence or abuse.

DOMESTIC VIOLENCE STARTS SMALL—AND GROWS

Domestic violence rarely starts with an act of violence or physical assault—that would drive the victim away. Instead it is characterized by controlling behaviors that escalate incrementally over time. It may start as show of concern for the well-being of another. This is a normal behavior within a relationship. However, it may increase to include demands to know where the partner is, who they are with, what time they will be home. It may progress to more aggressive behaviors: a putdown, a look, sarcasm, a pretend blow, verbal or emotional abuse, aggressive behavior, or intimidation. These are designed to make the victim fearful. This controlling behavior can progress slowly or rapidly as the perpetrator tests the victim's reactions and tolerance to their abuse. Ultimately it may progress to include physical assault, sexual assault, threats of and actual death.

There may be anger when the abuser is drinking alcohol or using drugs or when the victim says "no" to them. This behavior can progress to physical or sexual assault, isolation, and death.

While many women will end the relationship with the first incident like this and leave, others become shocked, frightened, or embarrassed and trapped. Some will blame themselves, believing that they did something to deserve what is happening to them, a belief reinforced by the perpetrator.[41a,42]

BOILING THE FROG

Abusive partners rarely begin a relationship showing their abusive traits. Most times it happens slowly, incrementally. A good analogy is to compare it to boiling a frog. You do it slowly or else they'll jump out of the pot.

However, when you add the heat gradually, by the time the frog realizes what is happening, it's too late. So too it is for the victim of domestic violence.

DATING VIOLENCE

Unhealthy relationships can start early and last a lifetime. Dating violence often starts with teasing and name calling. These behaviors are often thought to be a "normal" part of a relationship. But these behaviors can set the stage for more serious violence like physical assault and rape.

Teen dating violence is defined as the physical, sexual, or psychological/emotional violence within a dating relationship, as well as stalking. Stalking can occur in person or through electronic means and may occur between a current or former dating partner. It is a form of domestic violence.

Adolescents and adults are often unaware that teens experience dating violence. In a nationwide survey:

- **9.4 percent of high school students report being hit, slapped, or physically hurt on purpose by their boyfriend or girlfriend in the twelve months prior to the survey.**[43]
- About one in five women and nearly one in seven men who ever experienced rape, physical violence, and/or stalking by an intimate partner, first experienced some form of partner violence between eleven and seventeen years of age.[44]

INDICATORS OF DOMESTIC VIOLENCE CAN BE SEEN EARLY IN A RELATIONSHIP

The pathway to domestic violence starts early in a relationship. The initial behaviors are innocent enough and are part of our relationship development rituals as we show concern about the other person. **It may comprise, for example, possessiveness, wanting to be with a person all the time, wanting to know where they are, who they are with.**

These behaviors leave the realm of normal when the intensity ratchets up and it becomes controlling—wanting to know where the person is all the time, what time they got home last night, who they were with. Early in a relationship, this pattern may not be obvious—even to the victim.

These more intense behaviors are indicators of the true personality behind the abuser and are red flags that they may escalate and worsen as the relationship develops. Before the partner knows it, they can be drawn deeply into a relationship that they find difficult to get out of, if at all.[45]

Threats precede action. Some threats are a rehearsal for action. When we listen to what abusers are saying, they tell us what they intend to do. If they say, "I'm going to hit, smack, hurt, beat, or kill you," we shouldn't be surprised when they do.

IS THERE A WAY TO CHECK IF YOUR NEW PARTNER COULD BECOME ABUSIVE?

The "No Test" suggests watching out for the way your partner responds the first time you change your mind or say "no." Watch their reaction.

While expressing disappointment is OK, it's not the same as annoyed. Annoyed is "How dare you!" a sign of ownership or entitlement.

The response that you receive is a good indicator of how your relationship will develop. If the response is overly negative, that may indicate that this relationship is not going to be a good one. Move on.[46]

DOMESTIC VIOLENCE, INTIMATE PARTNER VIOLENCE: RISK FACTORS

Persons with certain risk factors are more likely to become perpetrators or victims of domestic or intimate partner violence (IPV). Those risk factors contribute to domestic violence but might not be direct causes. Not everyone who is identified as at risk becomes involved in violence.

Some risk factors for domestic violence victimization and perpetration are the same, while others are associated with one another. For example, childhood physical or sexual victimization is a risk factor for future domestic violence perpetration and victimization.

A combination of individual, relational, community, and societal factors contribute to the risk of becoming a domestic violence perpetrator or victim. Understanding these factors can help identify various opportunities for prevention. One or many risk factors may be involved.

Risk Factors for Domestic Violence

Individual Risk Factors

- Low self-esteem
- Low income
- Low academic achievement
- Young age
- Childhood trauma
- Exposure to domestic violence as a child
- Aggressive or delinquent behavior as a youth
- Heavy alcohol and drug use
- Depression
- Anger and hostility
- Antisocial personality traits
- Borderline personality traits
- Prior history of being physically abusive
- Having few friends and being isolated from other people
- Unemployment
- Emotional dependence and insecurity
- Belief in strict gender roles (e.g., male dominance and aggression in relationships)
- Desire for power and control in relationships
- Perpetrating psychological aggression
- Being a victim of physical or psychological abuse (consistently one of the strongest predictors of perpetration)
- History of experiencing poor parenting as a child
- History of experiencing physical discipline as a child

Relationship Factors

- Marital conflict: fights, tension, and other struggles
- Marital instability: divorces or separations
- Dominance and control of the relationship by one partner over the other
- Economic stress (financial, poverty)
- Unhealthy family relationships and interactions

Community and Family Factors

- Poverty and associated factors (e.g., overcrowding)
- Unemployment
- Low social support: lack of institutions, relationships, and norms that shape a community's social interactions
- Weak family/friends, coworker, or community response to domestic violence (e.g., unwillingness to intervene in situations where they witness abuse/violence).[47]

6. Perpetrators of Domestic Violence

WHO DOES IT?

Perpetrators of domestic violence come from all socioeconomic, cultural, and educational backgrounds—as do victims. Perpetrators and victims of domestic violence are not the same, they differ. There is no typical victim. In hindsight it may be possible to highlight some common victim features that were not visible prior to the abusive relationship. Perpetrators may show distinct behavioral patterns—particularly cyclical offenders who follow a path to violence. Their behavior is predictable as they follow a cycle of tension building, violence, and reconciliation.[48,49,50]

The use of violence and abusive behaviors in a relationship is a behavioral modification tool. It is used by the perpetrator to control and manipulate the victim.

TYPES OF DOMESTIC ABUSER

1. *Constant:* This is a perpetrator who is constantly abusive—emotionally, verbally, physically or sexually—inside and outside the home. **Their violence, or threat of violence, is instrumental—it is designed to achieve a distinct purpose; that of maintaining power and control over their partner**. Abuse or violence for them is a means to get what they want, when they want it. They are abusive by nature, lacking in conscience. They enjoy the terrorizing and harm they cause. They may be cold and calculating in what they do.[51]

2. *Cyclical:* The cyclical abuser follows a predictable behaviorally abusive and conciliatory path. That is not to say that the onset of their abusive behavior is predicable; it may not be. As many victims know, abusers like these can get upset quickly or their abusive behavioral outbursts occur over time. Once the abuse commences, how the abuser behaves follows a predicable path. Their violent behavior is generally kept to inside the home. They are careful not to show this behavior outside the home; it is kept just for those they victimize. Often friends or coworkers will disbelieve that this person is capable of violence

when they hear of it—they can be a "nice guy" when they want to.[52,53]

Perpetrators of violence only use tactics that work for them; what is controlling of one victim might not have the same effect on another.

Note: For a more in-depth discussion on the types of abusers and the abusive mentality, the book *Why Does He Do That?* by Lundy Bancroft is recommended.

Traits of Domestically Violent Men and Their Female Victims

According to the World Health Organization, **men are more likely to perpetrate violence if they have low education, a history of child maltreatment, exposure to domestic violence against their mothers, harmful use of alcohol, unequal gender norms including attitudes accepting of violence, and a sense of entitlement over women.**

Women are more likely to experience domestic violence if they have low education, exposure to mothers being abused by a partner, abuse during childhood, and attitudes accepting violence, male privilege, and women's subordinate status.[54]

Men with more traditional, rigid, and misogynistic gender-role attitudes are more likely to practice marital violence.[55] **There is a consistent relationship between men's adherence to sexist, patriarchal, and/or sexually hostile attitudes and their use of violence against women.**

PERPETRATOR MANIPULATIONS

Grooming

"Grooming" is the methodical, intentional process of manipulating a person to gain their trust to a point where they can be victimized. It is a tactic of overcoming the victim's defenses by slowly desensitizing their natural reactions to abusive behaviors.

Most relationships that become violent or controlling do not start that way. Instead they often begin with romance and friendship; this is the beginning of the grooming process. Abusers may shower their future victims with attention, flattery and care. The abuser may initially seem the ideal companion—devoted, loving, supportive—wanting to spend every minute with their new partner. This flood of romance can feel overpoweringly positive, leaving the recipient in an altered state where reality may seem suspended. This is a predatory tactic that is meant to build a deep emotional connection. Abusers know exactly what they are doing.

Part of what they do is to slowly convince their victim that they—the abuser—are the only one in the world who really cares about them.

After establishing a foundation of trust and care, abusers will then start to make requests of the victim to judge how far they can push their boundaries of control. Romantic gestures can abruptly turn into intimidation. Abusers typically blame their partners for growing tensions. Victims will work hard to appease the abuser, trying to keep themselves safe and get back to the early romantic intensity. Incremental abuse desensitizes the victim to what is happening to them. **Desensitization** works hand in hand with the illusion of developing a special relationship. This is produced by a mix of positive reinforcements, simulated affection, and controlling behaviors resulting in a bond developing between the victim and the abuser referred to as a "trauma bond" (see page 107).

Attempts to **isolate** the victim leads them to believe that there are no other options. The more an abuser can isolate an individual from their support networks, the easier it is for the abuser to remain in control. The relationship is sprinkled with acts of kindness which keeps the affection that the victim has for their abuser from disappearing. It also keeps them in the hope that the person that they fell in love with still exists.[56,57]

When we hear the word "grooming" we think of sexual offenders who target children. However, grooming comes in many forms. For most of us the process of grooming is the normal means by which we interact with others throughout the day including attracting partners; we present our best selves to others in the hope of getting people to like us and to achieve our goals.

In situations of domestic violence these grooming skills are important for the perpetrator in attracting, retaining and controlling their victim.

Grooming Others

Perpetrators also attempt to manipulate others around them—friends, neighbors, family members, coworkers—into believing, for example, that the perpetrator is incapable of treating his partner or family member in the way that they are accused.

If they are arrested and appear before a judge these grooming techniques are used to try and convince the judge, jury, therapists, case managers and other professionals that they, the perpetrators, are the real victim; that *they* are not capable of doing what they are accused of; the real issue, they will say, is with the victim.[58]

Manipulating the Legal System

As professionals—law enforcement, social services, the court—become involved with a family, the abusive partner may look for ways to get these individuals to collude with them against the victim. In some cases, perpetrators actively employ the legal system as a means of maintaining ongoing control of their victims. The offender may:

- Present themselves as the victim.
- Present the victim as a bad parent.
- File for divorce or threaten to.
- File a lawsuit against the victim.
- Use convincing statements of remorse or guilt as a way to avoid consequences.
- Describe the protective actions by the victim (e.g., leaving, defending themselves, or calling law enforcement) as ways to make them look bad, get an advantage in court, or hurt them.
- Present as the more stable and calmer partner (e.g., using the victim's anger/distress about the situation as an example, while they remain calm and cooperative).
- Deny or minimize their actions (e.g., "She bruises easily" or "I just pushed her a little," or "She did it to herself to make me look bad").
- Avoid responsibility by blaming alcohol or other substances, stress, etc.
- Allege that the partner is an alcoholic or chemically dependent.
- Allege the partner has mental illness.
- Present themselves as the provider for the family, both financially

and emotionally.
- Present the victim's behavior in a negative way to get others to side with the perpetrator.
- Present the victim parent as the barrier to resolving the family's problems (e.g., they won't go to counseling), while presenting themselves as the good parent who wants to keep the family together.
- Presenting their own behaviors as being misunderstood (e.g., he is protective of her).[59]

Perpetrator's Manipulations While Arrested or in Jail

Research illustrates that in many cases the arrested perpetrator may reach out to their victim while they are incarcerated or after an arrest to groom/manipulate the victim to drop or recant the charges. The perpetrator appeals to the victim's sympathy through descriptions of their suffering from mental and physical problems, illness, intolerable jail conditions, and life without the victim.

Perpetrators often use a system that minimizes the violent behavior while gaining the victim's sympathy and trust. This plays on the victim's emotions, causing them to later recant their previous statements about the assault. The intent is to make the victim feel badly about the charges that the perpetrator is facing and for the victim to, in turn, agree to help the perpetrator get the criminal case dismissed.

This system includes tactics such as:

- not allowing the victim to talk about the abuse with others,
- resisting responsibility,
- denying credibility of the victim's story, and,
- reminding the victim that they—not the abuser—were to blame for the violence.[60]

Most perpetrators do not see their behaviors as acts of domestic violence. Their sense of privilege is such that they consider their controlling behaviors to be right—and even necessary—to ensure that others fulfill their expectations. They choose not to see that their behaviors cause fear and harm.

They are, however, very aware of others' use of violence and are very quick to detail others' actions against them, while denying or downplaying their own.

There is a tendency by people who have used violence and abuse as a pattern of coercion to identify as a victim when they experience any act of violence toward them.

See "Misuse of the Legal System Against the Victim" on page 83 and "A Word of Warning for Victims" on page 104.

Men who do admit to using violence often try to justify or downplay their violence, or to blame their partner—perhaps for "provoking" an attack or giving them "no way out." They might refer to their partner as being oversensitive, irrational, hysterical, a danger to themselves, or even mentally ill when trying to minimize their own behavior to others.[61]

Power is the critical dynamic in domestically violent relationships. This means that while it is usually perpetrated by men against women and children, domestic violence can also be perpetrated in other ways—for example, in LGBTQ⁺ relationships, by a child or adolescent toward a sibling or parent, by an adult son or daughter toward their parent, or by a caregiver toward a person with a disability.[62]

LIES AND RATIONALIZATIONS PERPETRATORS USE

Perpetrators often tell lies about their violence to themselves, their partners, and society:

"I just need to be understood."
"I had a bad childhood."
"I can't control it."
"I get angry."
"She/he (the victim) fights, too."
"She/he pushes my buttons."
"If I don't control her/him, she/he will control me."
"My smashing things isn't abusive, it's venting."
"I have a lot of stress in my life."
"I just have an anger management problem."
"I only have a problem when I drink or use drugs."[63]

Gaslighting or Psychological Manipulation

DEFINITION: To manipulate (someone) by psychological means into doubting their own sanity.[64]

Psychological and emotional abuse is an attack on the victim's personality rather than their body, and it can be just as harmful as physical abuse.[65]

Gaslighting is a term used to describe a form of psychological manipulation that seeks to sow seeds of doubt in a victim making them question their own memory, perception, and sanity. By using persistent denial, misdirection, contradiction, and lying, the perpetrator attempts to destabilize the victim and delegitimize the victim's belief. The abuser attempts to invalidate the victim's experiences using dismissive language, for example saying: "You're crazy. Don't be so sensitive. Don't be paranoid. I was just joking! . . . I'm worried; I think you're not well." The psychological manipulation may include making the victim question their own memory, perception, and sanity.

Examples may range from the denial by an abuser that previous abusive incidents ever occurred, up to the staging of bizarre events by the abuser with the intention of disorienting the victim.

The gaslighting behaviors of the abuser can be detrimental to the victim providing a formula for mental health issues for the victim, up to and including a nervous breakdown (severe, major, clinical depression), and possibly suicide.[66,67,68]

There are two characteristics of gaslighting: The abuser wants full control of feelings, thoughts, or actions of the victim, and the abuser discreetly emotionally abuses the victim in hostile, abusive, or coercive ways.[69]

Signs of gaslighting include:

- Withholding information from victim
- Countering information to fit the abuser's perspective
- Discounting information
- Verbal abuse, usually in the form of jokes or sarcasm
- Blocking and diverting the victim's attention from outside sources
- Trivializing the victim's worth

- Undermining victim by gradually weakening them and their thought process[70]

Three most common methods of gaslighting are:

1. **Hiding:** The abuser may hide things from the victim and cover up what they have done. Instead of feeling ashamed, the abuser may convince the victim to doubt their own beliefs about the situation and turn the blame on themselves.
2. **Changing:** The abuser feels the need to change something about the victim. Whether it be the way the victim dresses or acts, they want the victim to mold into their fantasy. If the victim does not comply, the abuser may convince the victim that he or she is not good enough.
3. **Control:** The abuser may want to fully control and have power over the victim. In doing so, the abuser will try to seclude them from other friends and family where only they can influence the victim's thoughts and actions. The abuser gets pleasure from knowing the victim is being fully controlled by them.[71]

A last word: Many abusers manipulate their victims carefully and purposefully. They switch easily between being charming and kind to raging and abusive and back again. To an outsider, the perpetrator may appear to be the perfect, caring partner. For the victim, the more a person is filled with doubt, the easier it is to control them.[72]

CHARACTERISTICS OF SOME PERPETRATORS OF DOMESTIC VIOLENCE

The following characteristics were identified by victims of domestic violence as behaviors exhibited by their partners. These traits may flag a new partner as a potential abuser. Many of these behaviors become visible early in the relationship.

- ***They are jealous and lack trust.*** They are extremely jealous and over-possessive. They don't trust their partner and, for example, expect them to immediately answer their texts, calls, or emails. They want to know why their partner doesn't answer right away.

- ***They need immediate gratification.*** They have strong needs that must be met right away; they expect their partners to dedicate themselves to those needs.
- ***They deny responsibility for their actions.*** This denial perpetuates the abuse, and over time intensifies it. They blame the victim and others for what they do.
- ***They are very rigid.*** They have rigid rules for behavior and use consequences to control their partner so that they follow these rules. When victims break a rule, they are "punished," physically or psychologically, or both. The "rules" don't apply to the abuser's behavior.
- ***They feel self-pity.*** They feel everyone else is at fault for their life, so they feel sorry for themselves. They feel nobody understands their potential or problems and feel that they are one against the world. Since others do not always make special concessions for them, they always disappoint them.
- ***Their selfish attitude towards their children and partner.*** Although they say that they love their children, the children rarely come first. **They expect the entire household to revolve around them.** If anyone steps out of line, their partner is to blame. Since they believe that their partner is responsible for their well-being, they expect them to know what they need without being asked.
- ***They isolate their partner.*** Perpetrators claim that their partner's family doesn't like them. They tell their partner that their friends and neighbors are "interfering." To increase their control over their partner, they do not allow them to see or talk to family or friends, thus isolating them from anyone who can help them.[73,74,75,76]

VIOLENCE IS A LEARNED BEHAVIOR

Domestic violence is a learned behavior—learned by a child through observation, experience, and reinforcement generally before the age of ten.[77]

It is learned from many facets of our society:

- from a parent/in the family—the primary source
- in the community—schools, peer groups, religious and cultural groups

and their attitudes toward the role of women
- in culture—music, movies, TV, video games

These lead to the objectification of the victim by the perpetrator.

VIOLENCE IS A SEPARATE BEHAVIOR

Domestic violence is not caused by genetics, illness, alcohol or drugs, anger, stress, the behavior of the victim or the dynamics of the relationship. It may be exacerbated by some of these issues but they are not the cause. The use of **violence**—the willingness to use violence to control another—is a separate and distinct behavior, and has to be addressed as such.[78,79]

DOMESTIC VIOLENCE IS A CHOICE ON THE PART OF THE PERPETRATOR

Abusers are able to control their behavior—they do it all the time.

- *Abusers pick and choose whom to abuse.* They don't insult, threaten, or assault everyone in their life who gives them grief. Usually, they save their abuse for the people closest to them, the ones they claim to love.
- *Abusers carefully choose when and where to abuse.* They control themselves until no one else is around to see their abusive behavior. They may act as though everything is fine in public, but lash out instantly as soon as they are alone with the victim.
- *Abusers are able to stop their abusive behavior when it benefits them.* Most abusers are not out of control. In fact, they're able to immediately stop their abusive behavior when it's to their advantage to do so (for example, when law enforcement show up or a neighbor calls at the door).
- *Violent abusers usually direct their blows where they won't show.* Rather than acting out in a mindless rage, many physically violent abusers carefully aim their kicks and punches where the bruises and marks won't show. Perpetrators will do all they can to blame the victim for the violence though intimidation, minimizing, denying, and direct blaming.

- *Perpetrators will appear outside the home as "nice guys,"* and their friends may express disbelief on hearing about violence.[80]

CAN AN ABUSER CHANGE?

Once an abuser has had all the power in a relationship, it can be **difficult to change** to a healthy relationship with equal power and compromises. **Sometimes, the abuser will stop the physical violence but may continue the verbal and emotional abuse.** The bottom line is that an abuser can change only if they are held **fully accountable, accept responsibility**—and the consequences—for their actions, and **make the choice** to change their behaviors.[81]

PROGRAMS DESIGNED TO HELP PERPETRATORS OF DOMESTIC VIOLENCE

A perpetrator will only change their behavior if they choose to do so. Nobody can make them change other than themselves.

The difficulties faced in treatment programs may start with the perpetrator blaming the victim for the abuse or excusing their own behavior through rationalization. **Anger management classes are ineffective because during an abusive episode anger calms the perpetrator—it is a release for them. Research shows that most partner-abusive men do not present with anger-related disturbances.**[82]

The goals of treatment have to include making the perpetrator rethink how they view the victim, to see them as a person rather than an object. They have to unlearn their behaviors toward the victim and their attitudes toward them—behaviors and attitudes often learned and ingrained from childhood.

Batterers Intervention Program (BIP)

Batterers intervention programs are designed to help perpetrators **change their behavior and to develop respectful, non-abusive relationships**.

The emphasis is on taking responsibility for violent and abusive behavior, without minimizing it or blaming others. Perpetrators learn that they are in control of their own behavior and can choose not to be violent. It is important that they understand the impact of violence and abuse on their partner and their children.

They learn different, non-abusive ways of dealing with difficulties in intimate relationships. Changing behavior is a long-term process, especially for someone long habituated to the use of violence and other forms of abuse. Perpetrators are most frequently motivated to change their violent behavior when they are brought to recognize its destructive impact on their **children**.[83]

Why Not Anger Management Classes?

Batterer Intervention Program educational content which focuses on anger and the development of anger management skills is inappropriate. Anger management does not challenge or explain the value system supporting domination and violence and creates the mistaken assumption that loss of emotional control is the cause of domestic abuse. The anger management model fails to explain or confront the batterer's selective targeting of abuse and may serve to increase the batterer's skills in nonphysical control over others. Some stress or anger management techniques may be presented as part of a BIP program if **it is emphasized that anger or other emotions are not at the root of battering. Anger is used as a controlling technique which, if ineffective, escalates into violence.** Learning to reduce stress and manage anger does not necessarily reduce a batterer's belief that domination of a partner is not appropriate.[83]

The key to change is the decision—a choice—to change. No program can make that happen; it's up to the individual.

Why Not Couples Counseling for Abusive Relationships?

Therapy can be very effective for some couples who are working through difficult relationship issues. According to the National Domestic Violence (NDV) Hotline, **if abuse is present in the relationship, couples counselling is *not* recommended**.

To ensure that couples counseling is successful, both partners must be willing to take responsibility for their actions and be willing to adjust their behavior. Abusive people want all the power and control in the relationship and will focus on maintaining that imbalance, even if it means continuing unhealthy and hurtful behavior patterns.

Many callers to the NDV Hotline have related stories of trying and failing at couples counseling because of an abusive partner's focus on manipulating the sessions to place blame, minimize the abuse, and attempt to win over the therapist to their side.

If the therapist tries to hold the abusive partner accountable for these tactics, the abuser will often refuse to attend further sessions and may even forbid their partner to see the "biased" therapist again. The abusive partner may even choose to escalate the abuse because they feel their power and control is being threatened.

Abuse is not a relationship problem. Couples counseling may imply that both partners contribute to the abusive behavior, when, in fact, the choice to be abusive lies solely with the abusive partner.[84]

Batterer Intervention Program Is a 6-Month Intensive Program

This program works only if the abuser chooses to change. BIPs are designed to address the root causes of domestic violence and prevent participants from committing acts of domestic violence in the future. It consists of an initial assessment, orientation, and at least twenty-six weeks of group counseling sessions.

The curriculum used may include the following components:

- An educational approach that assigns **responsibility** for the violence solely to the batterer and provides a strategy for assisting the batterer in taking responsibility for the violence;
- Content that encourages the participant to develop **critical thinking skills** that will allow the participant to rethink their behavior and identify behavior choices other than violence;
- **Content that supports the belief that domestic violence is primarily a learned behavior**;
- Content that supports the belief that domestic violence is **not provoked or the result of substance abuse**;
- Content designed to improve the batterer's ability to **identify and articulate feelings**;
- Content designed to improve communication skills and listening with **empathy**;
- Content designed to improve negotiation and conflict resolution skills;
- **Content that challenges stereotypical gender-role expectations**;
- Content that includes strategies for helping the batterer to develop and improve support systems;

- Content that identifies the effects of distorted thinking on emotions and behavior;
- Content that identifies the effects of domestic violence on children;
- Content that includes information on the relationship of substance abuse to domestic violence.[85]

Therapy

Unless the therapist is an experienced and **qualified domestic-violence trained counselor,** therapy is not recommended. The perpetrator will attempt to **manipulate the therapist** into believing that the issues at home are due to their lack of self-esteem, mental health issues, problems with the victim or the family. Nothing can be gained for the victim by such therapy.

Abusers Who Pose a Particularly Severe Risk

Although domestic violence perpetrators often share more similarities than differences, it is not useful to categorize them. Attempts to divide perpetrators into typologies have not proven useful in terms of assessing or treating them.[86]

However, there is a category of domestic violence perpetrator—approximately 10–20 percent—who have particularly severe histories of using family and domestic violence that are somewhat distinct from the majority of perpetrators. These men might have significant criminal histories and are the most difficult to change through treatment.[86]

These men pose a particularly severe risk and require enhanced supervision, containment and monitoring from the civil and criminal justice systems.[86]

ONLY ONE PERSON CAN STOP THE VIOLENCE OR ABUSE

Only the perpetrator has the ability to stop the violence. Violence is a behavioral choice for which the perpetrator must be held accountable. Many victims make numerous attempts to change their own behavior in the hope that this will stop the abuse. This does not work. Changes in family members' behavior will not cause the perpetrator to be nonviolent or to stop the abuse.[87]

CONSEQUENCE FOR DOMESTIC VIOLENCE

OFFENDERS—INTERVENTION PROGRAMS OR JAIL?

Both. The lesson that violence is not acceptable behavior is reinforced by time spent in jail. A choice to change may be helped by intervention programs—or not.

7. The Domestic Violence Cycle

CYCLICAL ABUSE: THE CYCLE OF VIOLENCE WITHIN A RELATIONSHIP

Relationships are rarely always abusive although many are. A typical pattern is a cycle of violence. The cycle begins with a buildup of tension followed by an abusive or violent incident; afterwards there is a period of apology and reconnection and calm (the honeymoon period) when the victim may experience renewed hope in the relationship. They hope that this time the perpetrator will change, and that the violence will stop. It doesn't. In time the cycle begins again. As time passes the honeymoon period may disappear altogether and the cycle falls into a pattern of tension and violence. This pattern was first described by Lenore Walker in 1979.[88]

Tension: In the tension-building phase, the victim will begin to notice behavior changes in the abuser. Perhaps the abuser stops talking to them, they become moody or sullen, and nitpick the victim's behavior or other issues that annoy them. There may be threats made to the victim; they or their needs may be ignored, they may be made to feel that the tension is their fault. The perpetrator may isolate their partner further from those outside the family, withdraws affection, is verbally abusive, drinks and drugs, threatens, destroys property, and criticizes. The victim walks on eggshells to avoid the inevitable outburst that they know is coming.

Violence: The violence phase may be the escalation of the tension phase or it may be explosive—the smallest thing may trigger an outburst. Anything may happen—extreme verbal abuse, physical abuse, throwing objects, or attacking the victim, their children, or property directly—any type of violent behavior including sexual assault, rape, serious injury, threats of death or murder.

Honeymoon/reconciliation, calm period: This phase is a time where the abuser tries to make up with the victim. They are apologetic; they may present flowers, gifts, a trip, money. They beg forgiveness claiming they don't know what came over them. They promise to stop drinking; to go to treatment, to attend Alcoholics Anonymous (AA), Narcotics Anonymous (NA), to get counseling. It is during this time of reconciliation and calmness that the victim gathers hope that things may change. Change rarely happens.

Instead the honeymoon phase may become shorter and shorter until eventually it disappears completely, and the victim is left with a two-phase cycle of tension and violence.

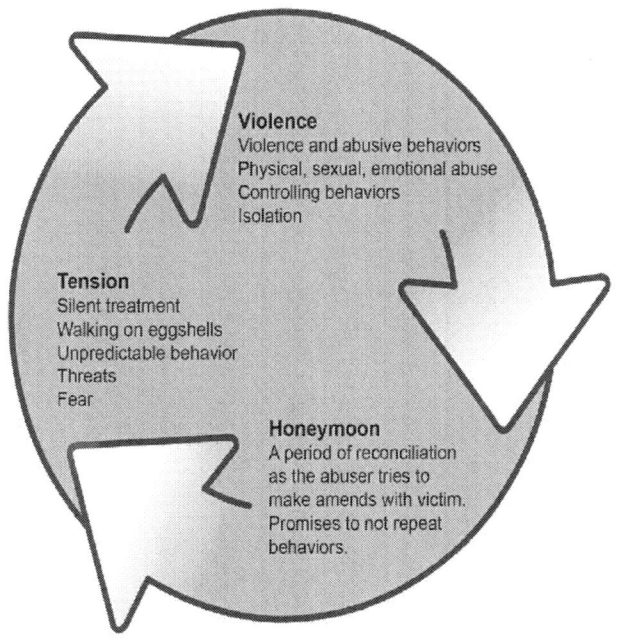

Violence
Violence and abusive behaviors
Physical, sexual, emotional abuse
Controlling behaviors
Isolation

Tension
Silent treatment
Walking on eggshells
Unpredictable behavior
Threats
Fear

Honeymoon
A period of reconciliation as the abuser tries to make amends with victim. Promises to not repeat behaviors.

The Cycle of Violence[91]

The cycle may happen frequently or infrequently—once a month for example, or once every few months, or once a week/day. Or many times a day.

The cycle will not stop until the perpetrator is arrested and jailed, the perpetrator or victim leaves the relationship, the perpetrator makes a decision to change their behavior through intervention, or either party dies.[89]

A Discussion about the Use of the Term 'Cycle of Abuse'

The pattern of abuse and term "cycle of abuse" was developed by Leona Walker in 1979. It is commonly used in courtrooms, with therapists and in the media. According to the National Domestic Violence Hotline (NDVA) there is resistance to using the term "cycle" for the following reasons.[90]

To describe abuse as a cycle implies that there are three or four predictable, repetitive steps of what is going on in any relationship at any given time:

1. Tension-building
2. Incident: abuser acts out—often a physical altercation
3. Reconciliation
4. Calm

According to the NDVA, if abuse was a cycle, it would be predictable; the victim would know what to expect and when to expect it. However, the reality about domestic violence is that it doesn't happen that way. While there may be recognizable patterns going on in a relationship (the victim recognizes abuser behaviors that lead to abuse or violence) the violence or abuse rarely occurs in a predictable cycle.

The NDVA does not use the term "cycle" because they believe that the term is at times used to blame victims for the continuation of abuse.

The Duluth Model of Power and Control

The model that describes what occurs in an abusive relationship is the Duluth Model and its Power and Control Wheel. It explains the many tactics an abusive partner uses at any one time to establish and maintain power and control over their partner. It was developed following intensive interviews with women who had been abused by men.

The Deluth Model of Power and Control Wheel

PHYSICAL VIOLENCE SEXUAL

Using Coercion and Threats
Making and/or carrying out threats to do something to hurt her, threatening to leave her, to commit suicide, to report her to welfare, making her drop charges, making her do illegal things.

Using Intimidation
Making her afraid by using looks, actions, gestures, smashing things, destroying her property, abusing pets, displaying weapons.

Using Emotional Abuse
Putting her down, making her feel bad about herself, calling her names, making her think she's crazy, playing mind games, humiliating her, making her feel guilty.

Using Isolation
Controlling what she does, who she sees and talks to, what she reads, where she goes; limiting her outside involvement, using jealousy to justify actions.

Minimizing, Denying, and Blaming
Making light of the abuse and not taking her concerns about it seriously, saying the abuse didn't happen, shifting responsibility for abusive behavior, saying she caused it.

Using Children
Making her feel guilty about the children, using the children to relay messages, using visitation to harass her, threatening to take the children away.

Using Male Privilege
Treating her like a servant, making all the big decisions, acting like "master of the castle," being the one to define men's and women's roles.

Using Economic Abuse
Preventing her from getting or keeping a job, making her ask for money, giving her an allowance, taking her money, not letting her know about or have access to family income.

POWER AND CONTROL

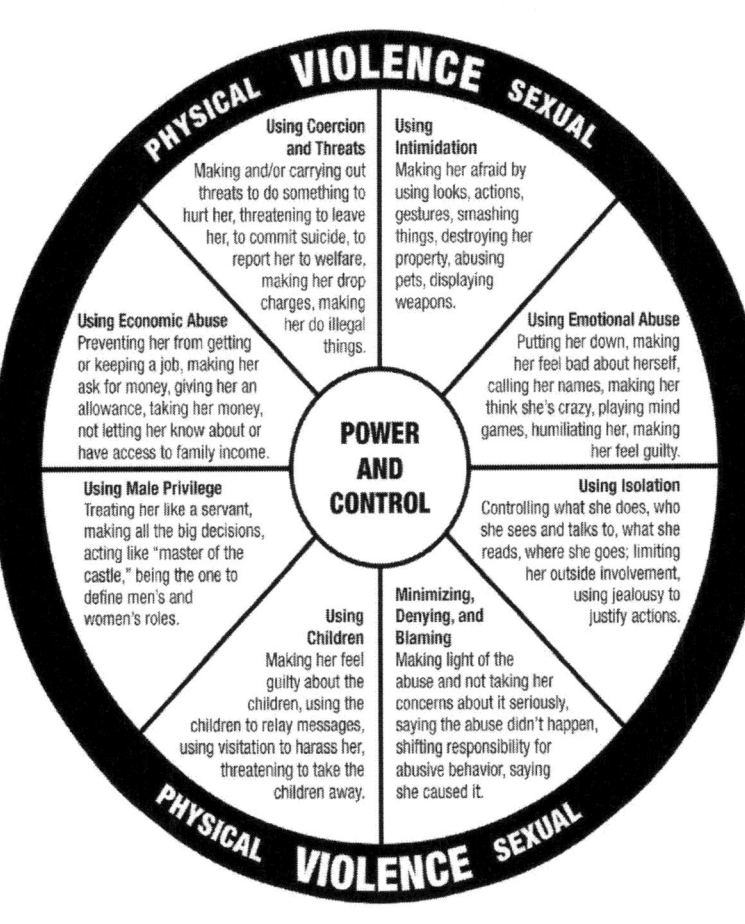

PHYSICAL VIOLENCE SEXUAL

The Deluth Model of Power and Control Wheel[92]

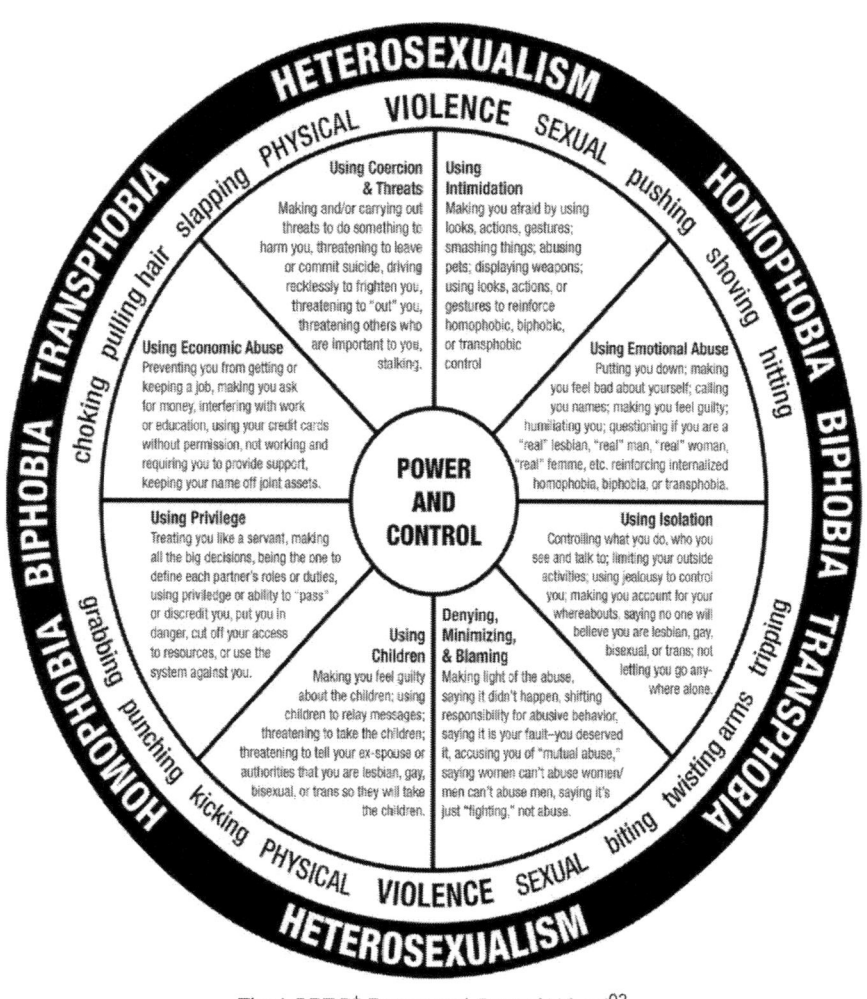

The LGBTQ+ Power and Control Wheel[93]

Outer ring
HETEROSEXUALISM · PHYSICAL VIOLENCE · SEXUAL · HOMOPHOBIA · BIPHOBIA · TRANSPHOBIA

Surrounding terms: slapping, pulling hair, choking, grabbing, punching, kicking, biting, twisting arms, tripping, gagging, hitting, showing, pushing

Center: POWER AND CONTROL

Using Coercion & Threats
Making and/or carrying out threats to do something to harm you, threatening to leave or commit suicide, driving recklessly to frighten you, threatening to "out" you, threatening others who are important to you, stalking.

Using Intimidation
Making you afraid by using looks, actions, gestures; smashing things; abusing pets; displaying weapons; using looks, actions, or gestures to reinforce homophobic, biphobic, or transphobic control.

Using Emotional Abuse
Putting you down; making you feel bad about yourself; calling you names; making you feel guilty; humiliating you; questioning if you are a "real" lesbian, "real" man, "real" woman, "real" femme, etc. reinforcing internalized homophobia, biphobia, or transphobia.

Using Isolation
Controlling what you do, who you see and talk to; limiting your outside activities; using jealousy to control you; making you account for your whereabouts, saying no one will believe you are lesbian, gay, bisexual, or trans; not letting you go anywhere alone.

Denying, Minimizing, & Blaming
Making light of the abuse, saying it didn't happen, shifting responsibility for abusive behavior, saying it is your fault—you deserved it, accusing you of "mutual abuse," saying women can't abuse women/men can't abuse men, saying it's just "fighting," not abuse.

Using Children
Making you feel guilty about the children; using children to relay messages; threatening to take the children; threatening to tell your ex-spouse or authorities that you are lesbian, gay, bisexual, or trans so they will take the children.

Using Privilege
Treating you like a servant, making all the big decisions, being the one to define each partner's roles or duties, using privilege or ability to "pass" or discredit you, put you in danger, cut off your access to resources, or use the system against you.

Using Economic Abuse
Preventing you from getting or keeping a job, making you ask for money, interfering with work or education, using your credit cards without permission, not working and requiring you to provide support, keeping your name off joint assets.

8. Victims of Abuse

THE CULTURAL MISTREATMENT OF WOMEN

While domestic violence describes more than just men-on-women violence, most of the reported abuse is directed at women by men.[94] The mistreatment of women by men is a worldwide problem that has been supported throughout history by many cultural, religious, and societal attitudes. This mind-set toward women is woven into the fabric of our lives through the media, music, tradition, pornography, and bias toward women that are passed on from generation to generation. The message is the same: it is the unspoken permission given for the mistreatment of girls and women.

Women are more likely to experience intimate partner violence if they have low education; exposure to mothers being abused by a partner; abuse during childhood; or attitudes accepting violence, male privilege, and women's subordinate status.[95]

LGBTQ+ relationships are not immune to intimate partner violence—it is reported that it occurs at the same rate among them as the general population.[96]

See Chapters 2 and 6 for more on perpetrators and victims.

TYPES OF VICTIMS

The person at whom the violence is aimed is referred to as the target victim. Others in the home, while the abuse is going on, or who are directly affected by the abuser, are referred to as secondary victims. Secondary victims include children, other family members, other adults, and pets. Everyone in the home is affected by the abuse and is at risk of potential harm.

VICTIM MENTAL HEALTH RESPONSES

Many victims of domestic violence, including adults and children who are exposed to it, develop mental-health problems as a result of their abuse. These include post-traumatic stress disorder, hyperarousal, anxiety, and other disorders. **This is a normal response to abnormal circumstances.** This is generally not an indication of inherent mental illness or personality disturbances in the victim. With adequate care and treatment in a safe environment these responses can be successfully addressed.

THE BEHAVIORS OF VICTIMS

Victims may be perceived as weak to others and may appear as though they are allowing the abuse to occur. Nothing could be further from the truth. In reality, they are actively trying to keep themselves and their children safe by doing whatever is necessary to appease the abuser.

At times these efforts may appear to be successful and they believe they can stop the violence, but over time, and as the violence escalates, they learn there is little or nothing they can do to stop it. They are coping the best they can.

Victims begin to believe they are helpless, a feeling reinforced by their abusers. Often, the victim does not use other strategies to try to end the violence, such as involving law enforcement or getting Orders of Protection because they believe it would result in an increased threat to them and their family. In many cases this is exactly what would happen.[97]

VICTIM BLAMING: BLAMING VICTIMS FOR THEIR OWN ABUSE

Adult victims tend to be blamed for their abuse because it is thought that, unlike abused children, they have options available to them in the face of their abuse. Many people think the adult victim contributes to their own victimization. Some believe that they are doing something to deserve or provoke the abuse or that in a perverse way, the victim enjoys it. **These views are generally not made about victims of other forms of violence.**

Social approval is more often given to a victim who resists rather than those who comply, even though resistance increases the likelihood of injury or death. Over time these victim-blaming views become incorporated into the victim's understanding of who they are.[98,99]

"WHY DON'T THEY JUST LEAVE?"

People who have never been abused often wonder why a person wouldn't just leave an abusive relationship. They don't understand that leaving can be more complicated than it seems.

Leaving is often the most dangerous time for a victim of abuse, because abuse is about power and control. When a victim leaves, they are taking

control and threatening the abusive partner's power, which could cause the abusive partner to retaliate in very destructive ways.

Aside from this danger, there are many reasons why people stay in abusive relationships. Here are just a few of the common ones:

- **Fear:** A person may be afraid of what will happen if they decide to leave the relationship.
- **Believing That Abuse Is Normal Behavior:** A person may not know what a healthy relationship looks like, perhaps from growing up in an environment where abuse was common, and they may not recognize that their relationship is unhealthy.
- **Hope That the Abuse or Violence Will Stop:** A victim's hope for the abuse to end is typically fueled by the perpetrator's promises to change. They may be subject to pleas from the children, from members of their community, church, or family to save the relationship, and other well-intentioned but misguided counsel. Victims hope that *this time* the perpetrator will actually stop what they are doing, unaware that without intervention (or even with intervention at times) that the chances are slim that the abuse will stop.
- **Embarrassment or Shame:** It's often difficult for someone to admit that they've been abused. They may feel they've done something wrong by becoming involved with an abusive partner. They may also worry that their friends and family will judge them.
- **Fear of Being Outed:** If someone is in an LGBTQ$^+$ relationship and has not yet come out to everyone, their partner may threaten to reveal this secret.
- **Low Self-Esteem:** When an abusive partner constantly puts someone down and blames them for the abuse, it can be easy for the victim to believe those statements and think that the abuse is their fault.
- **Love:** Many victims feel love for their abusive partner. They may have children with them and want to maintain their family. Abusive people can often be charming, especially at the beginning of a relationship, and the victim may hope that their partner will go back to being that person. **They may only want the violence to stop, not for the relationship to end completely.** Sporadic abuse interlaced with moments of kindness

keeps the hope alive in the victim that the abuse will stop; that their relationship with the abuser will revert to the loving connection that they had when they first met.

- **Children's Best Interest:** Some victims believe that it is in the children's best interest to have both parents in the home, particularly if the abuser does not physically assault the children. **The victims—and their attorneys, therapists, caseworkers, and judges—may not be aware of the serious impact that witnessing domestic violence has on children**, regardless of if they have been directly or physically abused by the perpetrator.
- **Cultural/Religious Reasons:** Traditional gender roles supported by the victim's culture or religion may influence them to stay rather than end the relationship for fear of bringing shame upon their family.
- **Language Barriers/Immigration Status:** If a person is undocumented, they may fear that reporting the abuse will affect their immigration status. Also, if their first language isn't English, it can be difficult to express the depth of their situation to others.
- **Lack of Money/Resources:** Financial abuse is common, and a victim may be financially dependent on their abusive partner. Without money, access to resources or even a place to go, it can seem impossible for them to leave the relationship.
- **Disability:** When someone is physically dependent on their abusive partner, they can feel that their well-being is connected to the relationship. This dependency could heavily influence their decision to stay in an abusive relationship.[100]

See "Leaving an Abusive Relationship."

HOW DOMESTIC VIOLENCE AFFECTS PEOPLE WITH DISABILITIES

The Americans With Disabilities Act (ADA) defines disability as "a physical or mental impairment that substantially limits one or more of the major life activities."

People with disabilities experience higher rates of domestic violence, sexual assault and abuse. Domestic violence can cause temporary or permanent disability.

In addition to other forms of abuse, a disabled victim of domestic violence or abuse may have a perpetrator who:

- Tells them that they are "not allowed" to have a pain flare up
- Steals or withholds their Social Security Disability check or other benefits
- Tells them that they are a bad parent or could never be a parent because they have a disability
- Uses gaslighting (psychological manipulation) to invalidate their disability (for example: "You're faking it" or "It's all in your head")
- Uses their disability to shame or humiliate them
- Refuses to help them use the bathroom or complete necessary life tasks
- Withholds or threatens to withhold medication; purposefully over-medicates them or mixes medications in a dangerous/non-prescribed way
- Steals their medicine
- Instigates sexual activity knowing that the disabled victim may not be capable of consenting or resisting
- Withholds, damages or breaks assistive devices
- Does not allow them to see a doctor
- Isolates them by not assisting them leave the home or access social technology
- Threatens to "out" their disability to others (for example, someone who is HIV-positive may not wish to disclose their status)
- Threatens to harm or harms their service animal
- Uses a disability as an excuse for the abuse; tells them that they "deserve" abuse because of their disability[100a]

Elder Abuse

Elder Abuse is an intentional act or failure to act that causes or creates a risk of harm to an older adult. An older adult is someone age 60 or over. Elder victims are subject to the same types of abuse as other victims. The abuse occurs at the hands of a caregiver or a person the elder trusts.[100b]

9. How Domestic Violence Affects Children

Domestic abuse can seriously harm children and young people. Witnessing domestic abuse is child abuse. Teenagers can suffer domestic violence in their own relationships.[101]

The risks to the mother are a direct predictor of the risk to the child. Increasing the safety of the adult victim will, in most cases, increase the safety of the child.[102,103]

THE LINK BETWEEN DOMESTIC VIOLENCE AND CHILD ABUSE

Domestic violence and child abuse go hand in hand. More than 50 percent of domestic violence–influenced households also have directly abused children.[104]

That only tells part of the story as a child does not have to be directly involved in a domestic violence incident to be hurt by it. **Being present in a home where there is domestic violence makes the child a witness. As a witness they are a participant and as a participant they are victims.**[104a] Therefore, children who are present during any incident of domestic violence are victims and may suffer consequences—physically, emotionally, or otherwise. These consequences can have far-reaching effects on the child, sometimes throughout their lives.

Witnessing violence between a child's parents or caregivers is the **strongest risk factor** for transmitting violent behavior from one generation to the next.[105,106]

Perpetrators of family and domestic violence harm children because of their controlling behaviors, sense of entitlement and self-centered attitudes. In order to keep child and adult victims safe, perpetrators of family and domestic violence must be held accountable for their actions and actively encouraged and supported to cease their violent behavior.[107]

EXPOSURE TO VIOLENCE AS A CHILD

Children learn behaviors through observing their parents or caregivers.

Directly observing, hearing, or learning about the abuse of another person (child, relative, caregiver, or individual) or a direct experience with abuse and neglect is the *strongest* predictor of domestic violence victimization as an adult and a strong predictor of perpetration as an adult.[108]

Very young children (ages 0–6) may be especially traumatized as a result of their exposure to violence. Even before they can talk, infants and young children are found to be sensitive and responsive to the fears and emotions of their caregivers and may suffer anxiety, increased aggressiveness, and developmental delays.[109,110]

Not all children exposed to violence are affected equally or in the same ways.

CHILDREN'S RESPONSES TO DOMESTIC VIOLENCE

Many factors influence children's responses to domestic violence. Not all children are equally affected. Some children do not show obvious signs of stress or have developed their own coping strategies. Others may be more affected. A child's age, experience, prior trauma history, and temperament all have an influence. For example, an adolescent who grew up in an atmosphere of repeated acts of violence may have different post-traumatic stress reactions than a twelve-year-old who witnessed a single violent fight. A six-year-old girl who saw her mother bleeding on the floor and feared she would die would likely have more severe reactions than a child who perceived the incident she witnessed to be less dangerous.

A child's proximity to the violence also makes a difference. Consider the very different experiences of a twelve-year-old child who was in another room with headphones on while her parents fought; an eight-year-old who had to call 911 despite a raging parent's threats against him; and a teenager who has frequently put himself at risk by getting into the middle of fights to protect his mother from her estranged boyfriend.

Here are some of the factors that can influence children's reactions to domestic violence:

- The severity of the violence (Was it life-threatening? Did the victim express terror in front of the child? Was a firearm or weapon used or brandished? Was there a serious injury?)
- The child's perception of the violence (A child may perceive violence

as life-threatening even if adults do not.)
- The age of the child
- The quality of the child's relationships with both parents (or involved parties)
- The child's trauma history (What other traumatic events has the child experienced? Was the child also a victim of physical abuse?)
- Secondary difficulties in the child's life, such as moving, changing schools, or leaving behind support systems[111]

Typical Short-term Responses of Children to Domestic Violence

Children commonly respond to domestic violence as they do to other traumatic events. Short-term traumatic stress reactions include the following:

- **Hyperarousal.** The child may become jumpy, nervous, or easily startled. They may live in a constant state of anticipation of another violent event.
- **Re-experiencing.** The child may continue to see or relive images, sensations, or memories of the domestic violence despite trying to put them out of mind.
- **Avoidance.** The child may avoid situations, people, and reminders associated with the violence, or may try not to think or talk about it.
- **Withdrawal.** The child may feel numb, frozen, or shut down, or may feel and act as if cut off from normal life and other people.
- **Reactions to reminders**. The child may react to any reminder of the domestic violence. Sights, smells, tastes, sounds, words, things, places, emotions, even other people can become linked in the child's mind with the traumatic events.
- **Trouble going to sleep or staying asleep** or having nightmares.
- **Repetitive talk or play about the domestic violence.** For example, a young girl may act out violence when playing with her dolls.

Other short-term symptoms may include anxiety (for example, separation anxiety); depression; aggression (perhaps reenactment of the witnessed aggression); physical complaints (stomachaches, headaches); behavioral problems (fighting, oppositional behavior, acting out observed behaviors, tantrums); feelings of guilt or self-blame; and poor academic performance.[112]

Children and Young People: Exposure to Domestic Violence

Exposure to domestic violence can be distressing, terrifying and frightening for a child, and causes serious harm. Children living in a home where domestic violence and abuse is happening are at risk of other types of abuse too. Children can experience domestic abuse or violence in lots of different ways. They might:

- See the abuse
- Hear the abuse from another room
- See a parent's injuries or distress afterwards
- Be hurt by being nearby or trying to stop the abuse

Children do not have to see the abuse to be affected by it.[113]

SYMPTOMS OF DOMESTIC VIOLENCE ON CHILDREN

Children are resilient yet growing up in a violent home can affect a child's life and development. **Research shows that nearly all children who live in homes where there is domestic violence, or who see or hear the abuse, are victims themselves as well.** The level of risk in each family varies and domestic violence can have a multitude of complicated effects on children. Symptoms experienced by children who have witnessed domestic violence can include:

- Sleep disorders
- Depression
- Mental health and emotional problems
- Bedwetting
- Impaired brain development
    - Learning problems
    - Stomachaches
    - Isolation from friends

- Truancy
- Problems at school

When properly identified and addressed, the effects of domestic violence on children can be lessened.

There is no typical way a child responds to domestic violence—each child is unique, as is their reaction to it. Many children have developed sophisticated strategies to protect themselves from being physically and emotionally harmed.

The way in which a child responds to the violence is based on a combination of their age, gender, temperament, level of involvement in the violence, understanding of the experience, coping skills, and availability of support systems—friends, relatives, and other adults. The impact of domestic violence on children is real but many children show considerable resiliency in the face of this violence. **Research demonstrates a critical connection between resiliency (the capacity to recover quickly from difficulties) and a strong relationship between the child and the victimized parent.**[114]

PERPETRATOR'S INFLUENCE ON CHILDREN

Abuser behavior can deprive children of their childhood. Experiencing domestic violence forces children to develop adult coping skills to survive, mentally and physically. These skills may include, for example, having to be attuned to the offender's moods to avoid conflict, becoming hypervigilant to detect impending outbursts or violence, and developing avoidance techniques to protect themselves, the adult victim, or siblings—even the family pet. It is not part of a child's normal development to have to develop these skills so early in life.[115]

UNDERMINING THE VICTIM'S ROLE AS A PARENT

The perpetrator exerts a strong influence over the children's relationship with the victimized parent. Victims of domestic violence may be undermined in their parenting role. The violence can corrode the victim parent's relationship with their children. Perpetrators of domestic violence may frustrate their (ex-)partners' parenting in ways both obvious and subtle.

A perpetrator may:

- Involve the children in further controlling or harming the victim (e.g., have the children monitor the victimized parent—what they do, where they go, who they are with);
- Sabotage the other parent's authority through constant criticism or negative remarks;
- Engage in activities with the children that the abused parent has forbidden;
- Destroy the children's belongings when the abused parent counters their authority;
- Tell the children that the victimized parent does not love or want them;
- Tell the children that the victimized parent is going to abandon them.

As a result of these deliberate and corrosive influences by the offender, some children may develop a closer bond with the offending parent than with the abused parent.[116]

CHILDREN LEARN FROM THE VIOLENCE

Children may adopt the attitudes that support domestic violence and begin to form similar behaviors of their own. For example, they may blame the victimized parent for the abuse and problems in the family, use violence to resolve conflicts, or inflict abuse (emotional or physical) on the victimized parent, siblings, or pets.

CHILDREN MAY IDENTIFY WITH THE ABUSER OR THE VICTIM

Children who grow up in violent households tend to identify with either the victim or the aggressor. Children who identify with the victim may harm themselves through deliberate self-injury, for example, by burning or cutting themselves. They often think they caused the fight and should have been able to stop it. Those who identify with the aggressor may express violent themes in play, eliminating less powerful figures. In real life they often are characterized as bullies. Identification with the aggressor may be the reason why child witnesses to violence are apt to be violent toward siblings, and why, after the abuser is gone, some children will begin to swear and lash out at the non-abusive parent.[117]

SIGNS OF DOMESTIC VIOLENCE ON CHILDREN

Emotional

- Feeling guilty for the abuse and for not stopping it
- Grieving for family and personal losses
- Confusion regarding conflicting feelings toward the parents
- Fearful of abandonment, expressing feelings, the unknown, or of personal injury
- Angry about the violence and the chaos in their lives
- Depressed, feeling helpless and powerless
- Embarrassed about events and dynamics at home

Cognitive

- Believe they are responsible for the violence
- Blame others for their own behaviors
- Believe that it is acceptable to hit people they care for to get what they want, to express their anger, to feel powerful, or to get others to meet their needs
- Have a low self-esteem originating from a sense of family powerlessness
- Do not ask for what they need, let alone what they want
- Do not trust
- Feel that getting angry is bad, because people get hurt
- Have rigid sexual stereotypes, for example, what it means to be a man, woman, husband, wife

Behavioral (often seen in opposite extremes)

- Act out versus withdraw
- Anger
- Overachiever versus underachiever
- Refusal to go to school
- Caretaking, more concern for others than self, behaving as a parent

substitute
- Aggressive versus passive
- Rigid defenses: aloof, sarcastic, defensive, black & white thinking
- Excessive attention-seeking—often using extreme behaviors
- Bedwetting and nightmares
- Out-of-control behavior, unable to set own limits or follow directions

Social

- Isolated from friends and relatives
- Relationships are frequently stormy, start intensely, end abruptly
- Difficulty in trusting, especially adults
- Poor conflict resolution and anger-management skills
- Excessive social involvement to avoid home life
- May be passive with peers, or bully peers
- Engage in exploitive relationships either as perpetrator or victim
- Play with peers gets exceedingly rough

Physical

- Somatic complaints (headaches, stomachaches)
- Nervous, anxious, and a short attention span
- Tired, lethargic
- Frequently ill
- Poor personal hygiene
- Desensitization to pain
- Regression in development (bedwetting, thumb sucking—depending on age)
- High-risk play and activities
- Self-harm: cutting, burning, hair-pulling, deliberate serious self-injuring, and others
- Suicidal ideation, attempts, or successful suicide[118]

FACTORS THAT HELP CHILDREN RECOVER FROM WITNESSING OR PARTICIPATING IN DOMESTIC VIOLENCE

Most children are resilient if given the proper help following traumatic events. Research has shown that the support of family and community are key to increasing children's capacity for resilience and in helping them to recover and thrive.

Crucial to a child's resiliency is the presence of a positive, caring, and protective adult in a child's life. Although a long-term relationship with a caregiver is best, even a brief relationship with one caring adult—a mentor, teacher, day-care provider, an advocate in a domestic violence shelter—can make an important difference.

Other protective factors for children:

- Access to positive social supports (religious organizations, clubs, sports, group activities, teachers, coaches, mentors, day care providers, and others)
- Average to above-average intellectual development with good attention and social skills
- Competence at doing something that attracts the praise and admiration of adults and peers
- Feelings of self-esteem and self-efficacy
- Religious affiliations, or spiritual beliefs that give meaning to life[119]

10. Signs of Domestic Violence and What to Do

SIGNS THAT A PERSON MAY BE A VICTIM OF DOMESTIC VIOLENCE

There are often warning signs that domestic violence is occurring in a household or a relationship. These warning signs can include:

- One partner **frequently checks up on the other** (by listening in on phone calls, constantly asking about whereabouts—verbally, by email, text, phone, calling a person at work all day, checking a person's car mileage, texts, voicemails).
- One partner **not allowing the other to have guests** over to the home when the other partner is not present. This can include family or friends.
- **Visible injuries** or attempts by the victim to cover or hide injuries.
- **One partner putting the other down** (name-calling, public or private humiliation, or making the other partner feel crazy).
- **Evidence of destruction of property** such as holes in walls, broken furniture, or doors and windows that do not latch.
- **One partner trying to control or isolate the other**—for example, by telling them not to see certain friends or family members, keeping them away from school or work, making them stay home when they want to go out.
- One partner acting jealously or possessively toward the other.
- One partner cutting off utilities or denying the other access to the telephone or Internet.
- One partner threatening to hurt the other partner, or that partner's friends, family members, or pets.
- One partner forcing the other to engage in sexual activities in ways or at times that are uncomfortable or against their will.
- Displaying anger in a way that scares the other partner or others.

- One partner has complete control of the household finances.
- One partner blaming the other for all of the family's problems.
- The use of dominating or intimidating body language.
- One partner minimizing or denying the concerns of the other.[120]

A lack of police incident reports or arrests is not an indication that domestic violence has not happened. Law enforcement is rarely involved with families where domestic violence is occurring. A fear of an escalation of violence is one reason why a victim may not call law enforcement.

When the police are called, victims may under-report domestic violence incidents for fear of a response from the perpetrator. For example, they may report property damage but deliberately not mention a physical assault, or they may minimize what happened.

RECOGNIZING THE WARNING SIGNS OF DOMESTIC VIOLENCE AND ABUSE

It is impossible to know with certainty what goes on behind closed doors, but there are some telltale signs and symptoms of domestic violence. If you witness any warning signs of abuse in a friend, family member, or coworker, take them seriously and find out how you can help them even if all you can do is listen to what they say. The first step is to ask them what's going on.

Warning signs of domestic abuse

People who are being abused may:

- Seem afraid or anxious to please their partner.
- Always vigilant to please partner at home or in company.
- Receive near-constant calls or texts from partner.
- Go along with everything their partner says and does.
- Are reluctant to—or cannot—socialize outside of work or at the weekends without partner.
- Check in often with their partner to report where they are and what they're doing.
- Receive frequent, harassing phone calls from their partner.

- Talk about their partner's temper, jealousy, or possessiveness.
- Defend the abusing partner.

Warning signs of physical violence

People who are being physically abused may:

- Make excuses for visible injuries from domestic violence, attributing them to accidents. Pay attention to facial injuries: bruises, cut lips, black eyes.
- Frequently miss work, school, or social occasions without explanation.
- Dress in clothing designed to hide bruises or scars (e.g. wearing long sleeves in the summer or sunglasses indoors).

Warning signs of isolation

People who are being isolated by their abuser may:

- Be restricted from seeing family and friends.
- Rarely go out in public without their partner.
- Have limited or no access to money, credit cards, or the car.
- Have limited money to take care of themselves.

The Psychological Warning Signs of Abuse

People who are being abused may:

- Have very low self-esteem, even if they used to be confident.
- Show major personality changes (e.g., an outgoing person may become anxious or withdrawn).
- Be depressed, anxious, or suicidal.[121]

Ignoring signs of domestic violence or child abuse is not a neutral action. It is an act of collusion with the perpetrator.

Possible Warning Signs of Domestic Violence in Pregnant Women

Evidence in the United States suggests that domestic violence during pregnancy is a risk factor for women's increased risk of being killed by an intimate partner. For example, an examination of police and medical examiner records in eleven U.S. cities showed that pregnancy significantly increased women's risk of becoming a victim of intimate partner homicide and that men who abuse their partners during pregnancy seem to be particularly dangerous and more likely to commit homicide.[121a]

An especially concerning form of physical violence during pregnancy is when abusive partners target a woman's abdomen, thereby not only hurting the women but also potentially jeopardizing the pregnancy.

Estimated domestic violence rates for pregnant women range from 3.9 to 8.3 percent.[122]

Medical care utilization

- Missed medical appointments
- Repeated visits to the doctor
- Regular medical visits for injuries
- Unscheduled visits to the doctor

Pregnancy

- Late entry into prenatal care
- Young maternal age
- History of abuse or assault
- Unintended pregnancy

Medical conditions

- Chronic pelvic pain
- Recurrent headaches
- Irritable bowel syndrome
- Vaginitis

Mental health

- History of suicide attempts
- Depression and anxiety

- Unhappiness about being pregnant
- Substance abuse

Screening for Domestic Violence by Domestic Healthcare Professionals

Domestic violence may exist in the absence of any obvious medical and behavioral warning signs, illustrating the importance of routine screening. Routine screening for domestic violence by medical professionals can save the life of a victim of abuse.[123] **Screening should be done without the accompanying partner or caregiver present.**

The American Medical Association recommends routine screening of all women patients in emergency, surgical, primary care, pediatric, prenatal, and mental health settings for domestic violence. In many states healthcare providers are mandated reporters of domestic violence to law enforcement.[124,125]

WHAT TO DO IF YOU SUSPECT DOMESTIC VIOLENCE

Say something—ask. Speak up if you suspect domestic violence or abuse. Expressing your concern will let the person know that you care and may even save their life.

Do:

- Ask if something is wrong and explain why you are asking.
- Express concern about whatever it is you have noticed that made you ask the question.
- Be quiet and listen to what they are saying.
- Offer help—know what community resources are available to help them.
- Support their decisions.

Don't:

- Come across as accusatory or judgmental.
- Seek an explanation of what happened.

- Wait for them to come to you.
- Pressure them.
- Place conditions on your support.
- Give advice.

Offer instead the domestic abuse hotline number:
National Domestic Violence Hotline at 1-800-799-SAFE (7233) or TTY 1-800-787-3224 or www.thehotline.org **(referrals to local resources available). In an emergency call 911.**

Also see HotPeachPages for an international directory of domestic violence agencies: www.hotpeachpages.net.

11. Leaving an Abusive Relationship

Victims experiencing abuse may decide that leaving the home is their only option. Statistics show that leaving is the most dangerous time for victims. Why? Because abuse is about power and control. When a victim leaves, they are taking back control and threatening the abusive partner's power, which could cause the abusive partner to retaliate in very destructive ways. Violence can escalate exponentially when victims try to leave, and threats are often made against the children. **Leaving is when a threat of death is at its highest. Of the women who are killed by their partners, 75 percent are killed after they have left the abusive relationship.**[126,127,128]

Planning ahead will allow the victim time to decide what they intend to do, where they will go and what they will need to bring with them. This is referred to as "safety planning."

SAFETY PLANNING

Safety planning is a course of action that victims of domestic violence put in place as a means to safeguard themselves and their children from danger. The strategy is to have decisions and plans made in advance so that in the event of an emergency, there are plans in place to avoid, escape from, or manage a threat to their safety.

Safety planning can also be done with children. Studies show that safety plans that address the needs of adult victims and their children *together* are more effective. The plans are more likely to be maintained by the family after the court or service providers are no longer involved.

As with any strategy, **safety plans do not guarantee safety**. They are a system to increase that safety. A safety plan must be realistic, simple, and age-appropriate when applied to children. A thorough safety plan can take several hours to develop. It does not necessarily have to be written down. It should, if possible, be **rehearsed**—when the abuser is out—to eliminate any unanticipated problems.

A safety plan might include:

- **Packing and hiding a bag** with important documents, a phone, clothes, car keys, and cash in the house or at a friend's or neighbor's

house where it can be accessed quickly.
- **Keeping copies of important documents** in a safe place outside the home.
- **Having a separate bank account** and debit/credit cards that the perpetrator is unaware of, and unable to access.
- **Informing trusted family, friends, or neighbors of the plan**, and asking them for help if needed.
- **Working out exactly how to leave the home** with the children and where they will go.
- **Having information on local domestic violence resources.**
- **Notifying the children's school and the victim's employer about the plan.**
- **Finding a safe place to stay and ultimately live.**[129]

Copies of important documents—birth certificates, bank statements, passports, Social Security cards, insurance information, marriage license, etc.—should be left with someone outside the home for safekeeping. Perpetrators will not provide easy access to them after the victim has left. These documents may be the last vestige of control they have over the victim.

The safety of a child's mother is vital to the safety of her children.

Safety Planning with Children

Planning for Violence in the Home

A safety plan should include ways that your children can stay and feel safe when violence is happening in your home. It's important to remember that if the violence is escalating, you should avoid running to the children because your partner may hurt them as well.

- **Teach your children** when and how to call 911 or your police emergency number, and what to say.
- **Instruct them** to leave the home if possible when things begin to escalate. Arrange in advance where they can go.
- Come up with a **code word** that you can say when they need to leave the home in case of an emergency—make sure that they know not to

tell others what the secret word means. It can also indicate another action such as, to go to their room, call 911 or a family member, or not to interfere in what is going on between the perpetrator and the victim.

- In the house: **identify a room** they can go to when they're afraid. Suggest something they can think about when they're scared.
- **Instruct them** to stay out of the kitchen, bathroom and other areas where there are items that could be used as weapons or where weapons are stored.
- **Teach them** that although they want to protect you, that they should **never intervene**.
- **Help them** to make a list of people that they are comfortable talking and expressing themselves to about what is happening in the home.
- **Enroll them in therapy or a counseling program** (local service providers often have children's programs available free or on a sliding payment scale if you do not have insurance).

Planning for After You Leave the Relationship

Leaving the relationship is the most dangerous time for the victim. Leaving does not mean that the victim and the abuser will never see each other again. **After separation, children may remain the permanent link between the perpetrator and the abused parent.** Unless the abusive parent has lost their parental rights or there is a restraining order in place separating them from their children, they are entitled to see their children on a regular basis. The time sharing may be determined by the court.

To increase your safety:

- Alert and talk to anyone you can about what's going on: school authorities like the counselor, receptionist, teachers and principal, sports instructors, school bus driver and other caretakers. If you have a protective order or restraining order, provide the school with a copy that indicates clearly who can pick up the children—and who cannot.
- Perhaps provide a code word to the school so that they will know you when you call or send someone to pick up the children.
- Provide a copy of the restraining order to your local police department and to the police wherever you work.

How to Talk to Your Children About What's Going On

- **Let your child know that what's happening is not their fault and that they didn't cause it.**
- Your child may have a good idea of what is going on in the home and have questions for you. Depending on how old they are, provide them with as much information as appropriate and safe to do so. If you are hurt, say so.
- Let them know how much you love them and that you support them no matter what.
- Tell them that you want to protect them and that you want everyone to be safe, so you have come up with a plan to use in case of emergencies.

Be aware that whatever you tell the child may be told by the child to the abusive partner.

It's important to remember that when you are safety planning with a child, they might tell this information to the abusive partner, which could make the situation more dangerous (for example, "Mom said to do this if you get angry." Or "Mommy is planning to move with us.") When talking about these plans with your child, use phrases such as "We're practicing what to do in an emergency," instead of "We're planning what you can do when Dad/Mom becomes violent." As already mentioned, when a child is with their other parent, they may be eager to please them; they are their parent after all, and they love them.

Planning for Unsupervised Visits

Unless the abusive partner has had their parental rights terminated or there is a restraining order in place prohibiting contact, they will be entitled to see their children at regular intervals. If you are concerned for your children's safety when they visit their other parent, developing a safety plan for while they are at their home can be beneficial.

- Brainstorm with your children (if they are old enough) to come up with ways that they can stay safe using the same model as you would for your own home. Have them identify where they can get to a phone, how to call you or the police, how they can leave the house, and who they can go to.

- If it's safe to do, send a cell phone with the children to be used in emergency situations. This can be used to call 911, a neighbor, or you if they need help.
- Be aware that the abusive parent will have a relationship with the children. They may ask the children about you. The child may be eager to please them. Be aware that whatever you tell the child may be repeated to the abusive partner.

Planning for Safe Child-Custody Exchanges

- Avoid exchanging custody at your home or your partner's home.
- Meet in a safe, public place such as a restaurant, a bank, the mall or other area with lots of cameras, or a police station.
- Bring a friend or relative with you to the exchanges or have them make the exchange.
- If possible, have your partner pick the children up from school at the end of the day after you drop them off in the morning—this eliminates the chances of seeing each other. If you have a restraining order in place this may not be possible.
- Make a personal emotional safety plan as well—think of something to do before the exchange to calm yourself if you are apprehensive prior to the exchange. Plan on doing something afterwards to focus on yourself or the children, such as going to a park or doing a fun activity.
- Be aware of your personal safety during the exchanges.[129,130]

If you have any questions about safety planning or want an advocate's help in developing a personalized safety plan for your child, call the National Domestic Violence Hotline at 1-800-799-SAFE (7233).

POST-SEPARATION VIOLENCE

Post-separation violence is common in domestic violence situations. Separation can serve to accelerate this violence and its intensity.

The best time for the victim to leave a domestically violent relationship is during the "honeymoon" or calm phase, when violence is at a minimum. The abuser may be less likely to suspect a departure during this time.

Domestic violence protection systems, service providers, and the community must be ready to address the ongoing possibility of harm that exists for victims of domestic violence when they are no longer residing, or involved, with their abusive partner.

Victims have reported that after separation, their former partners have stalked, harassed, verbally and emotionally abused, beaten, and sexually assaulted them. They have also been murdered or killed as part of a murder-suicide.

A very dangerous time for a victim and their children is when they are pursuing a restraining order, a divorce, or taking other steps to remove themselves from an abusive relationship.

Custody and visitation arrangements are potentially dangerous for both the abused parent and children. Post-separation acts of violence are not solely directed toward the former partner. Other targets commonly include children, the spouse's new partner, and individuals identified as supporting or aligning with the former partner.[131]

POST-SEPARATION PERPETRATOR TACTICS

The offending parent may use the following tactics—many of which involve the children—in order to try to retain power and control over the adult victim:

- Reporting the victim to authorities for alleged abuse of children or for mental health issues
- Applying for sole custody of the children
- **Withholding child support**
- Quitting a job or remaining underemployed in order to avoid paying child support
- Blaming: telling the children that they cannot be a family because of the victim
- Showing up unexpectedly to see the children
- Kidnapping the children and taking them to a new home
- Calling the victim constantly under the guise of talking to or about the children
- Talking about what the victimized parent did "wrong"

- Showering the children with gifts during visitations
- Undermining the victim parent's rules for the children
- Picking the children up at school without informing the abused parent beforehand
- Stalking the victim
- Keeping the children longer than agreed upon
- Asking children what the victimized parent is doing and who they are with or seeing
- **Criticizing, assaulting, or threatening the victim's new partner**
- Abusing their new partner in front of the children
- Blaming the victim for the relationship ending
- Threatening to take custody away from the victim if they do not agree to reconcile
- Telling the children that the victimized parent is an alcoholic, addict, or mentally ill
- Keeping court cases active by frequent filings
- Physically abusing the children and ordering them not to tell their mother
- Changing visitation plans without notice[132]

MISUSE OF THE LEGAL SYSTEM AGAINST THE VICTIM

Courts and professionals can inadvertently become tools for perpetrators to continue their abusive behavior. **The legal system can be used effectively by the perpetrator as a way to maintain control over a victim through continual litigation on child custody and visitation issues.** Perpetrators can attempt to intimidate their partners by threatening to take the children away (for example, by making false reports to the Department of Child and Family Services (or equivalent agency), kidnapping the children or maintaining ongoing litigation around custody or parent-child contact). **Responding to such actions can be emotionally and financially exhausting for victims.**[133,134]

A Restraining Order is only effective if the abuser abides by it.

Otherwise it just a piece of paper and offers no guarantee of safety on its own.

See "A Word of Warning for Victims" on page 104.

Victim Response in Court—Keep Records

One of the best tools in a courtroom for a victim is a notebook in which the victim records every event, every interaction, every detail, however small, associated with the abuser. In it they should record times, dates, the exact nature of what happened including threats, emails, phone calls, and in-person contact. Exact quotes of what was said should be written as such —"like this." Transcripts and printouts of texts and emails including date and time stamps are useful, as are recordings of threatening voicemails and phone calls. Witness statements are also important if someone else saw what happened. The victim should inform the court about the existence of the notebook directly or through their attorney. A copy and regular updates should be given to the attorney representing the victim. Needless to say, the original should be kept in a safe place. The notebook stands as to the reliability of the victim and creates a record of the abuser's behavior.[135]

In responding to accusations and complaints from the abuser, address each and every item with a full counter-response including details, times, dates, witnesses etc. The advice of an experienced domestic violence attorney is always recommended.[136]

See "Filing for a Domestic-Violence Restraining Order" on page 99

DOMESTIC VIOLENCE SHELTERS

Accessing and Staying at a Domestic Violence Shelter

If you need to leave your home in an emergency, you may need to stay at a shelter. Shelters exist all over the country and may be accessed by asking the local police department, a local domestic violence advocacy group, the courthouse, or the National Domestic Abuse Hotline (800-799-7233) for a referral. If you have time ahead of leaving your home, look up the location of your nearest shelter and how to contact them. Give them a call and tell them what's going on. Your local police department may have information on local refuges. See the Directory at the end of this section.

What Is a Shelter?

A domestic violence shelter, also known as a women's shelter, emergency shelter, women's refuge, or battered women's shelter, is a place of temporary refuge, protection and support for women and their children escaping domestic violence in all its forms. The term shelter also describes a location that is open to people of all genders who are at risk.

What to Expect if You Go to a Shelter

Every shelter is different. The following is generally what you can expect:

Safe, private location. Shelters and safe housing programs make everyone's safety their first priority. You may be asked to keep the location a secret. Entry by anyone other than a victim or staff may be protected by statute. In some states entry by anyone other than the victim and approved visitors may be a felony.

No fees. Shelters and safe housing programs are free.

Transportation. Most programs will provide transportation to a shelter or safe housing program. Many also offer residents bus passes and transportation to appointments, daycare and work.

Children's safety. Advocates will work with both you and your children offering support, information and parenting resources. Domestic violence programs are mandated reporters of child abuse.

Self-provided childcare. Your children will always be under your watch and care. Childcare may be provided during group meetings, therapy and other activities.

Help finding a safe place for your pet. Shelters will work with you to find a place for your pets to be cared for elsewhere. Some shelters may allow pets; most do not.

Confidentiality. Your information will be private and will not be shared with other agencies unless you give your written permission. You will be asked to honor the privacy of other program participants by not discussing their names or circumstances with anyone else.

Food, clothing, and toiletries. Shelters and safe housing programs will provide basic necessities for you and your family at no cost.

Sleeping arrangements. You may share common areas and might be asked to share a bedroom. In most shelters you will share the kitchen, common living areas, and bathrooms with other residents.

Laundry facilities. Shelters and safe housing programs usually have laundry facilities and provide guests with linens (sheets, towels and blankets).

Visitors. Visitors are generally not allowed in the shelter or safe housing program, but you can meet with your friends and family elsewhere.

Some programs:

- Allow you to bring your pets. Many **do not** so be sure to make arrangements for the pet(s) ahead of time.
- Have computers you can use to check your email and access online resources
- Offer free cell phones for 911 calls only

What to Expect if You Go to a Safe Housing Program

- **Your stay will be short-term.** Safe housing programs offer short stays.
- **You will have daily contact with an advocate.** Throughout your stay, advocates will work closely with you to help find a safe place to move on to. Advocates are available in person weekdays and by phone on weekends.
- **Options for moving on.** If you still need a safe place when your stay at the safe housing program ends, an advocate will try to assist you to find a longer-term shelter/housing and make every effort to provide transportation for you to get there.[137]

Find a domestic violence shelter: National Directory (https://www.domesticshelters.org) search by city or zip code, the National Domestic Violence Hotline (800 799-7233), or call your local police department for help and a referral. In an emergency, call 911.

HOW A PERPETRATOR CAN TRACK YOU

With so much technology available and in use by everyone every day, it can be easy for an abuser to keep track of a victim. **Assume that the abuser has put tracking devices in place and respond accordingly.**

The following reviews some, but not all, of the means of tracking with possible solutions. To determine the best methods of stopping being tracked check online for the resources to do so. Your local police department may also be able to advise you.

1. **Your phone:** Phones—and your phone's location—are easily tracked in several ways. If the abuser is the primary telephone account holder, the phone company may allow them to track the location of the phones on the account without the victim knowing. In addition, turning on location sharing or adding a hidden tracking app on the phone can allow the abuser to track a phone without the knowledge of the victim. Even if the victim is completely sure that the abuser cannot track them, they are still vulnerable through other phones in the household—for example, the children's—if the abuser has had access to the their phones. All of your calls, texts, and voice mails may be tracked.

    It is suggested that you get rid of the phones as soon as you leave. Get a new number and a new phone. Get new phones for the children.

2. **Tracking devices:** Small tracking devices are available that track individuals. Sold, for example, as a way of tracking your children or an item of property, these devices show exactly where they are located. They are small and easily concealed in a pocket or bag without the victim knowing that they are there. They can also be hidden in the children's property. A diligent search may find them.

3. **Tracking devices on a car:** Car trackers are either wired to the car's battery and provide continuous information as to the location of the car or they are battery powered and must have their batteries charged frequently. Cars are easily accessed when parked in the driveway, at work, or at a store. To determine if there is a tracking device, bring the car to a car shop to have it checked out or check around the car yourself. You can also have a private investigator scan the car for a transmitter.

    If the car is a lease and the abuser is the lease holder, the car may be tracked by the dealer or finance company.

    Devices that are hidden inside the car can listen in on cell phone calls and transmit them "live" as they occur. Others have a video capability. Check online to find an expert to locate them.

4. **Tracking through social media:** Anyone using social media leaves digital footprints. Be aware of location tagging by social media.

Victims should suspend their accounts for a time while leaving the home or block access to the abuser and anyone who they may use to contact them.

5. **Personal computer/laptop/tablet:** If you have a computer or tablet in the home that is, or has been, accessible by the abuser, every keystroke and all your searches will be available to them even if you delete them. If you are searching for information about domestic violence, a shelter, or anything to do with plans of leaving the household, it is best to do it on a computer outside the home—at the library or at a trusted friend's house.

12. Myths and Realities of Domestic Violence

MYTHS AND REALITIES ABOUT DOMESTIC VIOLENCE

There are common misconceptions about domestic violence. The following myths and realities highlight a few.

1. MYTH: If it was really that bad, the victim would leave the relationship.

REALITY: Many victims do leave their relationships—an average of five to seven times before they are able to leave permanently. Some do leave the first time abusive behavior occurs, never to return. It is a disservice to them to think of victims as helpless—they're not. Leaving is an extremely dangerous time for a victim when a threat of death is at its highest. Violence can escalate by up to 75 percent when victims try to leave, and threats are often made against the children.

Often, people who have not been abused by an intimate partner say that if their partner ever abused them they certainly would leave. **A person may stay in an abusive relationship for a multitude of reasons, including survival.** Victims may stay because of fear, hopelessness, shame, guilt, economic dependence, love, isolation, religious or cultural beliefs, homelessness, or fear of losing custody of their children.

Perpetrators prevent their partners from leaving by threatening to harm or kill themselves, the children, and the victim. Many victims recognize that if they take steps to leave, they risk the violence escalating against them and their children. Many of the worst injuries and deaths occur when victims of domestic violence try to leave. As many as 50 percent of perpetrators find their partners and continue to abuse and harass them after separation. Remaining in, or returning to an abusive relationship, may be a rational means of survival for some victims.

Even when the relationship is over and the victim leaves, the threat of violence or abuse continues. Courts may award visitation rights to both parties, which means that the relationship continues through the children—for example, when the parties meet to pick up or drop off the children.

2. MYTH: Even if they leave, they will just find another abusive relationship.

REALITY: Victims of domestic violence do not seek out or enjoy abuse. This attitude blames victims for their own victimization. While some victims may become involved with other partners who later begin to abuse them, there is no evidence that the majority of victims have this experience. Low self-esteem, childhood victimization, mental illness, and depression do not cause a person to be victimized. However, the effects of violence on the victim may include loss of self-esteem, the use of alcohol and drugs, post-traumatic stress symptoms, or depression.

3. MYTH: Victims care more about their abusers than their children.

REALITY: Most victims surviving in abusive relationships routinely act in conscious ways to protect their children and to minimize the abuse directed toward them. Research has shown that the non-abusing parent is often the strongest protective factor in the lives of children who are exposed to domestic violence. Victims will and often do resist abuse directed toward their children, including withstanding violence perpetuated on them, in order to ensure their children's safety. Many victims worry that if they leave, they may pay the price by losing custody of their children in court. This fear is especially real for victim parents who have physical disabilities or histories of mental illness, alcohol or substance abuse, or among victims who are less financially independent or less educated than their abusive partners.

4. MYTH: Perpetrators abuse their partners because of alcohol or drug abuse.

REALITY: Alcohol or substance abuse does not cause perpetrators of domestic violence to abuse their partners, although it is frequently used as **an excuse**. Alcohol and substance abuse may increase the frequency or severity of violent episodes. It may lower inhibitions, exacerbating a tendency toward violence already present. Rates of simultaneously occurring domestic violence and alcohol abuse vary from as low as 25 percent in some studies, to as high as 80 percent in others. **Alcohol or chemical dependency treatment will not stop someone from perpetrating violence; dependency and violence are two distinct problems that need to be addressed separately.**[138]

5. MYTH: Domestic violence happens only in low-income families.

REALITY: Domestic violence and abuse happens in all kinds of families, rich and poor, urban, suburban and rural, in every part of the country, in every racial, religious, cultural and age group.

6. MYTH: Domestic violence is an anger-control issue.

REALITY: Domestic violence has nothing to do with anger. Violence is a tool abusers use to get what they want. Abusers are in control because they can stop when someone knocks on the door or the phone rings; they often direct punches and kicks to parts of the body where the bruises are less likely to show; they don't abuse everyone who makes them "angry," but wait until there are no witnesses and abuse the ones they say they love.

7. MYTH: Most assaults are really just a couple of slaps and they are not really harmful.

REALITY: Domestic violence is the second leading cause of injury to all US women and is the leading cause of injury to American women 15 to 44 years old.[138a]

8. MYTH: Children are not at risk for being hurt or injured.

REALITY: Men who abuse their partners are more likely to abuse the children in the home. Domestic violence is the number-one predictor for child abuse.

9. MYTH: Boys who witness violence will grow up to be abusers.

REALITY: The majority of children, male and female, who witness domestic violence do not become abusers themselves. Studies have found that 30 percent of male children who witness violence in the home may become abusers as adults. This means that 70 percent do not become abusers and are committed to ending the cycle of violence in their lives.

FACT: Domestic violence is a crime, specifically assault and battery by one person against another. It is a crime for anyone to physically harm or harass another person.

FACT: Domestic violence may lead to murder. 50 percent of all women who are murdered are murdered by their husbands, ex-husbands, or domestic partners.[139,139a]

MYTHS ABOUT LGBTQ⁺ DOMESTIC VIOLENCE

1. MYTH: Domestic violence is mainly a "straight" issue and does not occur often in LGBTQ⁺ relationships.

TRUTH: Although many people believe that only straight women can be victims of domestic violence, domestic violence actually occurs in LGBTQ⁺ relationships at similar or higher rates than in the general population.

2. MYTH: Incidents of domestic violence are less severe in LGBTQ⁺ relationships than when it happens in straight relationships.

TRUTH: The abuse experienced by LGBTQ⁺ individuals can be equally or more damaging. Studies show that gay men and bisexual women are more likely to experience severe physical violence than their straight counterparts, including being beaten, burned, or choked.

3. Myth: Psychological violence, which includes name calling, insulting, humiliating or attempting to monitor, control or threaten a partner, is not as serious as physical or sexual violence.

TRUTH: Psychological violence can be an equally devastating form of abuse. In particular, threats to out another person's sexual orientation or gender identity as a means of control are unique to the LGBTQ⁺ community.

4. MYTH: The more masculine, bigger and/or stronger partner is typically the abuser.

TRUTH: Gender plays a significant role in perceiving and reporting instances of domestic violence. Many people "gender" the violence in LGBTQ⁺ relationships; for example, they may assume that the offender in a relationship is always the more masculine-presenting partner. However, domestic violence does not discriminate; it can impact or be perpetrated by any person regardless of their physical or personal attributes (e.g. size, gender expression, or age).

5. MYTH: It is easier for LGBTQ⁺ victims to leave abusive relationships than it is for their straight and/or married counterparts.

TRUTH: Regardless of the gender identity, sexual orientation or marital status of two people in a relationship, leaving an abusive partner is often a difficult and painful process. In fact, LGBTQ⁺ relationships may be harder to leave than straight relationships. Being in a LGBTQ⁺ relationship does not diminish that pain.[140–151]

13. How the Law Views Domestic Violence/Getting a Restraining Order

LEGAL DEFINITIONS
(These may vary from jurisdiction to jurisdiction)

Assault

An assault is an intentional, unlawful threat by word or act to do violence to the person by another, coupled with an apparent ability to do so, and doing some act which creates a well-founded fear in the other person that such violence is imminent.

Aggravated Assault

"Aggravated" means a weapon is involved in the assault. An aggravated assault is an assault:

- With a deadly weapon without intent to kill; or
- With an intent to commit a felony.
- This includes sexual relations with a person who is under the age of consent.

Factors which raise an assault to an aggravated assault typically include the use of a weapon, the status of the victim, the intent of the perpetrator, and the degree of injury caused.

Battery. Felony Battery

The offense of battery occurs when a person:

- Battery: actually and intentionally touches or strikes another person against the will of the other;
- Felony battery is defined as intentionally touching or striking another person against their will which causes great bodily harm, permanent disability, or permanent disfigurement.

Aggravated Battery

A person commits aggravated battery who, in committing battery includes

- The use of a deadly weapon,
- Battery in which serious bodily injury occurs or where there is an *intent* by the perpetrator to cause serious bodily harm,
- Battery involving a hate crime,
- Battery against a police officer, or
- Battery against a vulnerable person, such as a child or an elderly person.

Felonies and Misdemeanors

A misdemeanor is considered a crime of low seriousness, and a felony one of high seriousness. As a general rule when trying to determine the difference between a misdemeanor and a felony, you can look to the maximum potential jail time for the crime for the answer.

Misdemeanor: a crime punishable by one or more of the following: less than one year in the county jail, fine, probation, restitution or other punishment. The exact definition and penalty vary from state to state.

Felony: A person convicted in a court of law of a felony crime is known as a felon. The U.S. federal government defines a felony as a crime punishable by imprisonment in excess of one year or death. Federal law breaks down classifications for felonies using sentencing guidelines by the amount of prison time.

Class A felony—life imprisonment or the death penalty;

Class B felony—twenty-five or more years;

Class C felony—less than twenty-five years, but more than ten years;

Class D felony—less than ten years, bur more than five years; or

Class E felony—less than five years, but more than one year.

Felonies include but are not limited to the following: murder; rape; aggravated assault and/or battery; arson; robbery; burglary; child abuse, child sexual abuse; the manufacture, sale, distribution, or possession with intent to distribute child pornography; of certain types, and/or quantities of illegal drugs; possession of some drugs, grand larceny or grand theft, i.e., larceny or theft above a certain statutorily established value or quantity of goods; and vandalism on federal property. There are many more.

Loss of Firearms

The consequence of a conviction involving domestic violence or a felony includes the loss of some of the perpetrator's rights, including the right to own or possess a firearm. The penalty for a felon being found with a firearm is itself a felony that can carry with it a sentence of up to ten years in prison.

Lautenberg Amendment: The Lautenberg Amendment to the Gun Control Act of 1968, effective 30 September 1996, makes it a felony for those convicted of misdemeanor crimes of domestic violence to ship, transport, possess, or receive firearms or ammunition. The Amendment also makes it a felony to transfer a firearm or ammunition to an individual known, or reasonably believed, to have such a conviction. Military personnel are not exempt from the Lautenberg Amendment.

Under the Lautenberg Amendment the offender must fit one of the following criteria:

- Be a current or former spouse, parent, or guardian of the victim.
- Share a child in common with the victim.
- Be a current or former cohabitant with the victim as a spouse, parent, or guardian.
- Be similarly situated to a spouse, parent, or guardian of the victim.[152]

A conviction for a misdemeanor crime of domestic violence represents the third most-frequent reason for denial of an application to purchase a firearm by the FBI, after a felony conviction and an outstanding arrest warrant.[153]

Legal Representation

It is not necessary for a victim of domestic violence to have an attorney to file for a restraining order or to appear in court. An attorney would be beneficial but is not essential. If the victim does hire an attorney to represent them, it is important that the attorney is experienced in domestic violence law.

Pro-bono (free) domestic violence legal aid: If the victim does not have the financial means to hire an attorney, the court or courthouse may provide information as to where a pro-bono attorney may be sought. There may be local domestic violence advocacy organizations who offer free legal aid to victims; these can be found online. **There is legal information available online at the National Network to End Domestic Violence at https://nnedv.org.**

Victim Advocates

For victims of domestic violence, a victim advocate may be requested or appointed by the court. Victim advocates are professionals trained to support victims of domestic violence. Advocates offer victims information, emotional support, and help finding resources and filling out paperwork. Sometimes, advocates will attend court with victims. Advocates may also contact organizations, such as criminal justice or social service agencies, to get help or information for victims.

Filing for a Domestic-Violence Restraining Order

The law offers protection for victims of acts of domestic violence. That protection includes the right to file a petition for a Restraining Order against the person inflicting the violence or abuse. A domestic violence Restraining Order is a Court order issued to prevent the recurrence of acts of abuse by a perpetrator, ordering the perpetrator to do specific things or to stop doing specific things.

Please note that a Restraining Order, an Order of Protection, an Injunction, or a Protective Order describe the same thing. There may be a different term for it depending on where the victim lives.

Who can get a Restraining Order?

Victims of domestic violence or those who have reasonable cause to believe that they are in **immediate danger of becoming the victim of any act of domestic violence**, can apply for an Restraining Order against domestic violence.

Restraining orders against domestic violence protect you against family or household members. You can file a petition for a restraining order against domestic violence if the abuser is:

- your current or former spouse or partner.
- any person related to you by blood or marriage (such as your aunt, cousin or brother-in-law);

- any person who lives or has lived with you, as if they were part of the family. The law protects you against these people even if they are no longer living with you; or
- someone you have a child in common with, even if you have never lived together and never married that person.

Parents or relatives can also request a domestic violence restraining order if the facts show the required pattern of abuse. Parents and caregivers may file for an order on behalf of (OBO) a child.

For the purposes of getting a restraining order against domestic violence, "domestic violence" means any assault, aggravated assault, battery, aggravated battery, sexual assault, sexual battery, stalking, aggravated stalking, kidnapping, false imprisonment, or any criminal offense resulting in physical injury or death of one family or household member by another family or household member. This definition may vary depending on where you live.

How the judge determines if you are "in immediate danger of becoming a victim of domestic violence"

Even if you have not been physically assaulted, you can still qualify for a restraining order if the judge believes you are in immediate danger of becoming a victim of domestic violence. When deciding this, the judge will look at the following factors:

- The history between you and the perpetrator, including threats, harassment, stalking, and physical abuse;
- If the perpetrator has attempted to harm you or family members or individuals closely associated with you;
- If the perpetrator has threatened to conceal, kidnap, or harm your child;
- If the perpetrator has intentionally injured or killed a family pet;
- If the perpetrator has used, or has threatened to use, any weapons such as guns or knives against you;
- If the perpetrator has physically restrained you from leaving the home or calling law enforcement;
- If the perpetrator has a criminal history involving violence or the threat of violence;

- If there was a prior order of protection issued against the perpetrator;
- If the perpetrator has destroyed personal property of yours (e.g., telephone, clothing, or other items belonging to you);
- Whether the perpetrator has behaved in any other way that leads you to reasonably believe that you are in immediate danger of becoming a victim of domestic violence.

Where do I get a Restraining Order?

The places where you can apply for a domestic violence restraining order may vary depending on the state or county you live in. Generally, you can request a restraining order by filing a petition at your local courthouse. Sometimes, specific courts—such as a domestic violence or family court—may be the appropriate places to apply for a restraining order.

If you are facing immediate harm you should call 911 to contact the police. A law enforcement officer should be able to advise you about getting a domestic violence restraining order.

The process for the issuing of a Restraining Order

Please note that this process may vary depending on where you live. Check with your local court, domestic violence advocacy group or police department. Some jurisdictions have an Emergency Restraining Order which is similar to the Temporary Injunction as described here.

When you file a petition for protection against domestic violence, the court will consider giving you two types of injunctions:

- a temporary injunction (Temporary Restraining Order) and
- a final injunction (Permanent Restraining Order) for protection against domestic violence.

Temporary Injunction (Temporary Restraining Order)

The temporary injunction is a court order designed to provide you and your family members with **immediate protection** from the abuser.

As soon as you file your petition (petition: a formal application made to a court in writing that requests action on a certain matter) for protection against domestic violence, the clerk will give your petition to the judge. **If the judge decides that there is an immediate and present danger of domestic** violence, the judge will grant the temporary injunction.

You will not have to testify and the abuser does not need to be present. The judge will make the decision based only on the information in your petition so it is important to take the time to fill out the petition carefully.

The temporary injunction takes effect as soon as the abuser is served with (formally given) a copy of the order. This is called giving the abuser notice or having the abuser served with process.

The temporary injunction stays in effect for a certain number of days but won't last longer than 15 days (unless the judge grants a continuance of the hearing for "good cause" shown by either party.) Before the fixed time period ends, there will be a full hearing to decide whether to give you a final injunction.

The date for the full hearing will be set at the same time the judge makes the decision about the temporary injunction. The temporary injunction will last until the full hearing takes place.

Even if the judge denies you a temporary injunction, it does not necessarily mean you will be denied a final injunction. If the judge believes that there is no immediate and present danger of domestic violence, the judge is still supposed to set a hearing date for a final injunction where you will have a chance to better present your case. However, be sure to ask the judge for a hearing—sometimes judges don't automatically set a hearing date.

Final Injunction (Permanent Restraining Order)

At the full hearing, the judge will decide whether to give you a final injunction. At this hearing the judge will hear your complaint and consider testimony and evidence from both parties. Witness may be presented to the court.

The final injunction may have a set period that it will be in effect (for example, one year) or it may not have an expiration date and last indefinitely.

If there is no expiration date, either you or the abuser can file in court to modify (change) or dissolve (end) the injunction at any time and the judge will decide whether to grant the relief requested.[154]

Violation of a Restraining Order

A person who violates any of these orders has committed a criminal offence. They may be in contempt of court and be subject to civil or criminal penalties, including fines or incarceration.[154]

What to do when a Restraining Order is issued

Keep a copy on your person. Provide a copy to the local police department and the police department at your work, your workplace (if appropriate), your children's school and aftercare—wherever you believe that it would help protect you and your children. Remember that the order alone cannot protect you from someone who intends to hurt you.

Contact with the person against whom you have a restraining order

If the person against whom you have a restraining order attempts to contact you, for example, by text or email, **do not respond**. No contact means no contact. No texts, no email, no mail, no contact through a third party. Nothing. If you need to contact the other party for any legitimate reason, go through your attorney. Keep notes and screen shots of any attempted contact from the other person and provide them to your attorney or the court. Courts may have a court-approved email system through which the parties may communicate only as it relates to the children. Check with your courthouse or attorney.

A restraining order may only be a piece of paper, but it is nonetheless legally binding. This means that the restrained individual may face serious consequences for violating the order.

A Word of Warning for Victims

A restraining order can also be used against the victim. How? The abuser may file for a restraining order against the victim as part of their abusive behavior, or in anticipation of the victim filing one. If they do, and they can convince a judge that their complaint against the victim appears to be valid, the restraining order can be used to disrupt, perhaps destroy, the victim's life. If the victim is served with the court papers and does not respond to the complaint or does not show up in court, the abuser may get a permanent restraining order by default. That permanent restraining order may effectively terminate the victim's rights where the children are concerned.

Both temporary and permanent orders mean that the victim can be forced out of their home. They may lose access to their children; permanently. Therefore, it is vitally important for victims to be vigilant for, and to respond to, any court documents that they receive. It is equally important to turn up for all hearings.

See "Manipulating the Legal System" and "Misuse of the Legal Aystem

Against the Victim."

Contact Through Social Media

As digital communications and social media evolve, new means of potential contact between parties in a domestic violence case have emerged, even when there is a restraining order in place. Direct contact with a person protected by a restraining order on Twitter, Facebook, Snapchat, Instagram, and other social media platforms does violate the terms of the order. Defining what "contact" is on social media can be problematic when less direct contact is involved.

For example, is a "like" by a perpetrator on a victim's Facebook page contact? Does a perpetrator's post mentioning their love for the victim on a friend's social media page (a third party) constitute contact? How about when the perpetrator posts about the victim on his own social media page, to be seen by their own set of friends, which may include friends and family of the victim?

Courts are beginning to understand the impact of technology and social media. If a victim is exposed to any social contact that they perceive as means of contact by the abuser, it is recommended that they screen-shot, print and keep copies of the events and provide them to their attorney and the court for consideration as contact attempts by the abuser.[155]

Guardian ad Litem

When the case involves children, a Guardian ad Litem (GAL) may be appointed by the court. The Guardian ad Litem (which is called a CASA or Court-Appointed Special Advocate in some states) is appointed to investigate the case, ensure the safety of the children, represent the children's best interests (not their wishes), and provide the court with a report(s) accompanied by supporting documents and the Guardian's observations and recommendations. The Guardian is the eyes and ears of the judge and reports directly to them. They are a party to the case and are included in all hearings and court-related documents and correspondence. They provide testimony in court.

Guardian ad Litem are provided with a court order by the judge which allows them to access all aspects of the case as it relates to the children. On presentation of their court order they may have access to the children, speak to the family, interview anyone relevant to the case, access notes and reports from a wide range of professionals including doctors, therapists, law enforcement, hospitals, schools and others without the permission of the children's parents. All the information that they collect is kept confidential and provided only to the court and the parties prior to a hearing. The judge uses the information provided in formulating decisions as to the management and outcome of the case, particularly the portion of the order that deals with children.

14. Useful Terminology in Understanding Domestic Violence

USEFUL DOMESTIC VIOLENCE TERMINOLOGY

Violent Resistance/Self Defense

The victim uses violence as a means of protecting themselves or their children. In doing so they may injure the offender; the result can be that the victim can end up being arrested for assault or battery as opposed to their abuser.

Escalation

Escalation describes the process by which controlling behavior becomes more frequent, less disguised, more damaging, and closer to lethal over time. Escalation occurs, in part, because the feeling of being in control is never stable for the perpetrator.

Cinderella Effect

The Cinderella effect refers to the research-backed evidence of an increased risk of abuse and death of nonbiological children by stepparents and live-in partners.[156]

Trauma Bond

Traumatic bonding refers to strong emotional ties that develop between two persons where one person intermittently harasses, beats, threatens, abuses, or intimidates the other.[156a] Once a trauma bond is established it becomes extremely difficult for the victim to break free of the relationship. The victim may be mentally confused, upset, or exhausted as a result of excessive stress caused by the cycle of abuse, honeymoon, and tension, and the need to be hypervigilant to anticipate the abuser's actions. The trauma bond can persist even after the victim leaves the relationship, with it sometimes taking months, or even years, for them to completely break the bond.

Stockholm Syndrome

Stockholm syndrome is a phenomenon in which a hostage begins to identify with their captor. This also happens with victims of domestic violence or child abuse. Over time some victims may begin to identify with their abuser, sometimes to the point of defending them and their abusive actions. They are reacting not to the abuse itself but to perceived small acts of kindness shown to them by the abuser. A lack of abuse can be mistaken as an act of kindness.

Predominant Aggressor

The predominant aggressor is the person who poses the most serious ongoing threat in a domestic violence situation.

Victim Playing (also known as playing the victim, victim card, or self-victimization)

Victim playing in the context of domestic violence is where the offender claims that they are the real victim in the relationship. They attempt to shift the blame for their actions away from themselves to the victim. This is often seen in court.

Parental Alienation

Parental alienation describes the deliberate process of the psychological and emotional manipulation of a child, by one parent against the other, into showing unwarranted fear, disrespect or hostility towards a parent and/ or other family members. Its intent—and effect—is to attempt to destroy the relationship between a child and the alienated parent. It is a form of emotional abuse. It occurs in incidences of domestic violence, separation or divorce especially where court proceedings are involved. **It is a behavior that may be used by perpetrators of domestic violence.**

However

The behavior as described is a natural protective behavior shown by victims of domestic violence in protecting their children from a perpetrator. There is nothing sinister about wanting to protect the children. A victim may warn their children about the dangers of a violent or aggressive perpetrator in order to protect themselves and the children from harm.

In the courtroom the perpetrator may accuse the victim of parental alienation when in fact the behaviors are protective in nature. In insisting in describing them as alienation, it becomes an extension of the abuse behavior shown toward the victim.

Failure to Protect

Victim parents may find themselves accused of child abuse or neglect because they allegedly failed to protect the child(ren) from the abusive parent's abuse. Blaming the victim often fails to consider what efforts the abused parent made to remove the children from the violence or to protect them from the perpetrator.

Adult victims use all kinds of protective strategies that fail due to the perpetrators' behaviors and not their own behavior. Adult victims may be protective of their children, but their efforts alone may not have been enough to stop the perpetrator from harming the children from exposure to domestic violence or actual harm. **There is a risk that the children may be removed from the non-abusive parent by social services if there are indicators that they could have done something to protect the child but did not.** Such indicators include attempting to protect the perpetrator's identity or lying, concealing or failing to report the abuse, exposure to violence, or neglect of the child.

15. Domestic Violence Statistics

> We have to be very careful when citing statistical reports that we don't create the perception that anyone actually has a handle on the rate of domestic violence in America. The truth is, domestic violence is rampant and diverse, and it's still something no one wants to talk about.
> —Sheryl Cates, CEO, National Domestic Violence Hotline

Recording incidents of domestic violence is generally dependent on victim reporting, therefore, many statistics are an underestimate of reality.

- Domestic Violence Homicides Increasing. Why? According to one researcher, guns that are purchased and kept in the home, ostensibly for the purpose of self-defense, end up being used against a family member.[157]
- Women are at more risk of violence at home than on the street.[158]
- Most domestic violence (77%) occurred at or near the victim's home.[159]
- Domestic violence is the leading cause of injury to women between the ages of 15 and 44 in the United States, more than car accidents, muggings, and rapes combined.[160]
- Domestic violence accounts for 21% of all violent crime.[161]
- Women of all races are vulnerable to violence by an intimate partner.[162]
- Of women seeking medical assistance at emergency departments, 22% to 35% are there because of domestic violence.[163]
- Domestic violence occurs in homosexual and heterosexual relationships; 22% to 46% of people in the LGBTQ⁺ community experience some violence from their partners.[164]
- 60.8% of female stalking victims and 43.5% men reported being stalked by a current or former intimate partner.[165]

- The number-one lethally factor in an abusive relationship is threats of harm and possession of a firearm.[166]
- The presence of a gun in a domestic violence situation increases the risk of homicide by 500%.[167]
- More than two-thirds of victims murdered by a spouse or ex-spouse were killed by a gun.[168]
- In 2003–2012, most domestic violence did not involve a weapon (77%).[169]
- Black women were murdered at a rate nearly 2.5 times higher than white women.[170]
- Over 80% of men who killed or abused a female partner were problem drinkers in the year before the incident.[171]
- More than two-thirds of homicide and attempted homicide offenders were intoxicated at the time of the incident, compared to fewer than one-fourth of their victims.[172]
- Dating partners may commit more domestic abuse than spouses.[173]
- Most female victims of intimate-partner violence were previously victimized by the same offender, including 77% of females ages eighteen to twenty-four, 76% of females ages twenty-five to thirty-four, and 81% of females ages thirty-five to forty-nine.[174]

People with Disabilities

People with disabilities have a higher lifetime prevalence of experiencing abuse than people without disabilities.

A survey conducted by the Spectrum Institute Disability and Abuse Project found that 70% of respondents with disabilities experienced some form of abuse by an intimate partner, family member, caregiver, acquaintance or stranger. Of those:

- 87.2% experienced verbal/emotional abuse
- 50.6% experienced physical abuse
- 41.6% experienced sexual abuse
- 37.4% experienced neglect

- 31.5% experienced financial abuse
- 37.3% reported the abuse to law enforcement[175]

Elder Abuse

Approximately 1 in 10 Americans aged 60+ have experienced some form of elder abuse. Some estimates range as high as 5 million elders who are abused each year.

Abusers are both women and men. In almost 60% of elder abuse and neglect incidents, the perpetrator is a family member. Two-thirds of perpetrators are adult children or spouses.[176]

Domestic Violence and the LGBTQ⁺ Community

- 43.8% of lesbian women and 61.1% of bisexual women have experienced rape, physical violence, and/or stalking by an intimate partner at some point in their lifetime, as opposed to 35% of heterosexual women.
- 26% of gay men and 37.3% of bisexual men have experienced rape, physical violence, and/or stalking by an intimate partner in their lifetime, in comparison to 29% of heterosexual men.
- In a study of male same-sex relationships, only 26% of men called the police for assistance after experiencing near-lethal violence.
- In 2012, fewer than 5% of LGBTQ⁺ survivors of intimate partner violence sought Restraining Orders.
- Transgender victims are more likely to experience intimate partner violence in public, compared to those who do not identify as transgender.
- Bisexual victims are more likely to experience sexual violence, compared to people who do not identify as bisexual.
- LGBTQ⁺ Black/African American victims are more likely to experience physical intimate partner violence, compared to those who do not identify as Black/African American.
- LGBTQ⁺ white victims are more likely to experience sexual violence, compared to those who do not identify as white.

- LGBTQ⁺ victims on public assistance are more likely to experience intimate partner violence compared to those who are not on public assistance.[177]

The National Domestic Abuse Hotline number is 1-800-799-SAFE (7233). Help is available 24/7 and in over 170 languages. All calls are confidential and anonymous. Or contact them online at www.thehotline.org.

16. How and Where to Get Help Now

There are people waiting to help, just a phone call away. They are not only willing, they are happy to assist. They understand what victims are going through—all you have to do is to make the call.

Emergency: 911 or your local emergency number.

National Domestic Violence Hotline
Help is available 24/7 and in over 170 languages. All calls are confidential and anonymous.
1-800-799-SAFE (7233) • 1-800-787-3224 (TTY)
www.ndvh.org or www.thehotline.org

International Directory of Domestic Violence Agencies—HotPeachPages
International directly of abuse hotlines, shelters, refuges, crisis centers, and women's organizations. Plus domestic violence information in over 110 languages.
www.hotpeachpages.net

Find a domestic violence shelter
National Directory—search by city or zip code.
www.domesticshelters.org

National Teen Dating Abuse Helpline
1-866-331-9474 • 1-866-331-8453 TTY • Text loveisrespect
www.loveisrespect.org

Free legal aid is available in many cities—call your local domestic violence advocacy group or courthouse for details on how to request a pro-bono (free) attorney.

Rape, Abuse, and Incest National Network (RAINN)
1-800-656-HOPE (4673)
www.rainn.org

National Sexual Violence Resource Center (NSVRC)
1-877-739-3895
www.nsvrc.org

VictimConnect Resource Center
855-4-VICTIM (855-484-2846)
www.VictimConnect.org

For a comprehensive list of additional resources visit:
National Coalition Against Domestic Violence
https://ncadv.org/resources
800-799-7233 (SAFE) • 800-787-3224 (TTY)

National Network to End Domestic Violence (NNEDV)
They offer many resources for victims, including legal advice.
https://nnedv.org

National Indigenous Women's Resource Center
855-649-7299 (toll-free) • 406-477-3896
http://www.niwrc.org

Technology Safety & Privacy: A Toolkit
www.techsafety.org/resources-survivors

Resources

Other books by the author

Child abuse: What you need to know. (Parker Publishing)

Child Abuse. Prevention through understanding with John E. Wright, MD, FAAP (Parker Publishing)

Books by other authors

Why Does He Do That? Inside the minds of angry and controlling men. Lundy Bancroft

Not to People Like Us. Hidden abuse in upscale marriages. Susan Weitzman, Ph.D.

LGBTQ⁺ Intimate Partner Violence. Lessons for Policy, Practice, and Research. 1st Edition. Adam M. Messinger, Ph.D.

Coercive Control. Evan Stark

Gaslighting. Recognize Manipulative and Emotionally Abusive People—and Break Free. Stephanie Moulton Sarkis, Ph.D.

Video

The Crime of Domestic Violence: International Association of Chiefs of Police (IACP) domestic violence training video. *The Crime of Domestic Violence* was developed to present law enforcement and partners with information to strengthen the response to victims of domestic violence. https://youtu.be/c5dVPVqOTDI

References

Introduction

1. Source: Department for Child Protection (2013). *Perpetrator Accountability in Child Protection Practice: A resource for child protection workers about engaging and responding to perpetrators of family and domestic violence,* Perth Western Australia: Western Australian Government (Page 14: Failure to manage emotions (such as anger or stress). Retrieved from https://www.dcp.wa.gov.au/CrisisAndEmergency/FDV/Documents/Perpetrator%20Accountability%20i

2. Bancroft, L. *Why Does He Do That?* Berkley Books 2002

3. Adapted from Bancroft, L. *Why Does He Do That?* Berkley Books 2002. Pages 121–122)

Chapter 1

4. National Domestic Violence Hotline (NDVH). Retrieved from https://www.thehotline.org/is-this-abuse/abuse-defined

5. Child Welfare Information Gateway (2014). *Definitions of Domestic Violence.* Retrieved from https://www.childwelfare.gov/pubpdfs/defdomvio.pdf

6. US Dept of Justice: Office on Violence Against Women (OVW). Domestic Violence. https://www.justice.gov/ovw/domestic-violence

7. Centers for Disease Control and Prevention. Violence Prevention. Intimate Partner Violence: Definitions. Retrieved from: https://www.cdc.gov/violenceprevention/intimatepartnerviolence/definitions.html

8. Department of Justice: *Men Who Murder Their Families: What the Research Tells Us.* Bernie Auchter. https://www.ncjrs.gov/pdffiles1/nij/230412.pdf

9. Florida Coalition Against Domestic Violence. *Understanding Domestic Violence.* Retrieved from https://www.fcadv.org/about/understanding-domestic-violence

10. Florida Coalition Against Domestic Violence. *Understanding Domestic Violence.* Retrieved from https://www.fcadv.org/about/understanding-domestic-violence

Chapter 2

11. Center for Disease Control. *The national Intimate Partner and Sexual Violence Survey.* 2010 Summary Report Page 2.

12. National Society for the Prevention of Cruelty to Children. Retrieved from: https://www.nspcc.org.uk/preventing-abuse/child-abuse-and-neglect/domestic-abuse/

13. BBC/CDC/Northwestern. Kelly, J. *Is violence more common in same-sex relationships?* Retrieved from: https://www.bbc.co.uk/news/magazine-29994648

14. Center for Disease Control 2010. CDC. *National Intimate Partner and Sexual Violence Survey.* Retrieved from: https://www.cdc.gov/violenceprevention/pdf/nisvs_report2010-a.pdf. Page 48). https://www.cdc.gov/mmwr/preview/mmwrhtml/ss6308a1.htm?s_cid=ss6308a1_e#Table6

15. *The Number of Male Domestic Abuse Victims Is Shockingly High—So Why Don't We Hear About Them?* Birch, J. 2015. Retrieved from: https://www.yahoo.com/lifestyle/the-number-of-male-domestic-1284479771263030.html

16. Center for Disease Control 2010. CDC. *National Intimate Partner and Sexual Violence Survey.* Retrieved from: https://www.cdc.gov/violenceprevention/pdf/nisvs_report2010-a.pdf. Page 48)

17. Adapted from: *The Number of Male Domestic Abuse Victims Is Shockingly High—So Why Don't We Hear About Them?* Birch, J. 2015. Retrieved from: https://www.yahoo.com/lifestyle/the-number-of-male-domestic-1284479771263030.html

18. Adapted from National Coalition Against Domestic Violence. *Domestic Violence and the LGBTQ+ Community.* https://ncadv.org/blog/posts/domestic-violence-and-the-LGBTQ+-community

19. National Coalition of Anti-Violence Programs. (2006) *"Anti-Lesbian, Gay, Bisexual and Transgender Violence in 2006."* www.ncavp.org and http://avp.org/wp-content/uploads/2017/04/2006_NCAVP_HV_Report.pdf]

20. Adapted from New York State Office for the Prevention of Domestic Violence. *Domestic Violence in the Lesbian/Gay/Bisexual/Transgender/Queer Community.* https://opdv.ny.gov/whatisdv/LGBTQ+dvinfo.pdf

21. Adapted from New York State Office for the Prevention of Domestic Violence. *Domestic Violence in the Lesbian/Gay/Bisexual/Transgender/Queer Community.* https://opdv.ny.gov/whatisdv/LGBTQ+dvinfo.pdf

22. Adapted from National Coalition Against Domestic Violence. *Domestic Violence and the LGBTQ+ Community.* https://ncadv.org/blog/posts/domestic-violence-and-the-LGBTQ+-community

Chapter 3

23. Center for Disease Control and Prevention (CDC). 2013 (last reviewed). "Intimate Partner Violence: Definitions." Retrieved from: www.cdc.gov/violenceprevention/intimatepartnerviolence/definitions.html

24. Livet Dye, M. and Davis, K. 2003. "Stalking and Psychological Abuse: Common factors and relationship-Specific Characteristics." Violence & Victims 18(2):163–180. Department of Psychology, University of South Carolina. Available as a pdf at https://people.cas.sc.edu/daviske/dye davisarticle.pdf

25. Adapted from *Stalking Resource Center*. The National Center for the Victims of Crime. Retrieved from: https://victimsofcrime.org/our-programs/stalking-resource-center/stalking-information/#what

26. Daly, E. 2013, "Domestic abuse types rarely occur in isolation" (illustration) from *Child abuse: What you need to know.* (Amazon/Parker Publishing).

27. Abrahams, H. 2007. *Supporting Women after Domestic Violence: Loss, Trauma and Recovery.* London and Philadelphia: Jessica Kingsley Publishers.

28. Dutton, M. A. 1992. *Women's Response to Battering: Assessment and Intervention.* New York: Springer.

Chapter 4

29. Campbell, J. C., et al. 2003. "Assessing Risk Factors for Intimate Partner Homicide." *NIJ Journal 250* (November), NCJ 196547. Also See: NYS Office for the Prevention of Domestic Violence. Retrieved from https://www.ncjrs.gov/pdffiles1/jr000250e.pdf

30. Kellermann, A. L., Rivara, F. P., Rushforth, N. B., et al. 1993. "Gun Ownership as a Risk Factor for Homicide in the Home." *New England Journal of Medicine 329*(15):1084–1091. Retrieved from www.jhsph.edu/research/centers-and-institutes/johns-hopkins-center-for-gun-policy-and-research/publications/IPV_Guns.pdf

31. Violence Policy Center (VPC). 2009. "When Men Murder Women. An Analysis of 2009 Homicide Data," (p. 3). Data submitted for the FBI Supplementary Homicide Report. Per report, "In 2009, there were 1,818 females murdered by males in single victim/single offender incidents. Data does not include

Florida. 63 percent (989) of female homicide victims were wives or intimate acquaintances of their killers." Retrieved at www.vpc.org/studies/wmmw2011.pdf

32. Jacquelyn C. Campbell, et al., "Risk Factors for Femicide in Abusive Relationships: Results from a Multisite Case Control Study, '93 Am. J. Pub. Health (July 2003): 1089, 1092. Retrieved from: https://www.ncbi.nlm.nih.gov/pmc/articles/PMC1447915/pdf/0931089.pdf

33. Moracco KE, Runyan CW. Femicide in North Carolina, 1991–1993. Homicide Stud. 1998;2:422–447. Retrieved from (subscription needed): https://journals.sagepub.com/doi/10.1177/1088767998002004005

34. Adams, David. *Why Do They Kill?* Men Who Murder Their Intimate Partners. Retrieved from https://www.ncjrs.gov/pdffiles1/nij/230412.pdf

35. Hon Judge Alan F. Pendleton (ret). Minnesota Judicial Training and Education Blog. *Bail hearings in felony strangulation cases: Seven medical-legal faces every judge should know (14-07)* https://pendletonupdates.com/2014/05/05/bail-felony-strangulation/ (also Gael B. Strack, JD, CEO and Co-Founder of the Family Justice Center Alliance, San Diego, CA; Dr. Michael Weaver, M.D., Medical Director, St. Luke's Hospital's Sexual Assault Treatment center, Kansas City, Missouri)

36. Geanacopoulos, P. 1999. *Domestic Violence: A training manual for the Greek Orthodox Community*, " Page 7. Retrieved from https://www.scribd.com/document/259090061/DOMESTIC-VIOLENCE-A-Training-Manual-for-the-Greek-Orthodox-Community

37. National Coalition against Domestic Violence (NCADV). *Pregnancy and Domestic Violence Facts.* Retrieved from https://www.uua.org/sites/live-new.uua.org/files/documents/ncadv/dv_pregnancy.pdf

37a Homicide-Followed-by-Suicide Incidents Involving Child Victims. Joseph E. Logan, PhD, MHS, Behavioral Scientist, Sabrina Walsh, DrPH, Assistant Professor, Nimeshkumar Patel, MA, IT Specialist, System Analyst and Data Manager, and Jeffrey E. Hall, PhD, MSPH, Behavioral Scientist. https://www.ncbi.nlm.nih.gov/pmc/articles/PMC4699178/

38. National Institute of Justice. Auchter, Bernie. *Men who murder their families.* Retrieved from: https://www.ncjrs.gov/pdffiles1/nij/230412.pdf

39. Adapted from: Domestic Violence Survivors at Higher Risk for Suicide. Domesticshelters.org. Retrieved from: https://www.domesticshelters.org/articles/health/domestic-violence-survivors-at-higher-risk-for-suicide

40. National Center for Biotechnology Information, U.S. National Library of Medicine. Courtenay E. Cavanaugh, Ph.D., Jill Theresa Messing, M.S.W., Ph.D., Melissa Del-Colle, M.S.W., Ph.D., Chris O'Sullivan, Ph.D., and Jacquelyn C. Campbell, Ph.D., RN, FAAN. *Prevalence and Correlates of Suicidal Behavior among Adult Female Victims of Intimate Partner Violence.* Retrieved from https://www.ncbi.nlm.nih.gov/pmc/articles/PMC3152586/#R1

41. Department of Justice's Community Oriented Policing Services (Cops) Retrieved from: https://www.theguardian.com/us-news/2016/jul/31/police-officer-fatalies-department-of-justice-report

Chapter 5

41a. Adapted from New Choices. n.d. "*Domestic Violence.* Retrieved from: https://newchoicesinc.org/domestic-violence/

42. Adapted from Mayo Clinic: *Domestic violence against women: Recognize patterns, seek help* https://www.mayoclinic.org/healthy-lifestyle/adult-health/in-depth/domestic-violence/art-20048397

43. The National Domestic Violence Hotline. Retrieved from https://www.thehotline.org/resources/statistics/

44. CDC. The National Intimate Partner and Sexual Violence Survey | 2010 Summary Report. *Violence by an Intimate Partner.* Page 59. https://www.cdc.gov/violenceprevention/pdf/nisvs_report2010-a.pdf

45. RAINN (Rape, Abuse & Incest National Network). *Sexual assault. Early Warning Signs of Dating Violence.* https://www.rainn.org/news/early-warning-signs-dating-violence

46. Andrews, Rob. Adapted from *Domestic violence and a simple tool called the 'No Test' could identify an abusive partner.* ABC.Net Australia. Retrieved from https://www.abc.net.au/news/2019-01-31/how-the-no-test-could-helpprevent-domestic-violence/10764100?fbclid=IwAR0EWb42wWv7FJREHlOY-bPV8WWuR_lUFinkWoC_EX2riO-OVgJNp08ow8I&pfmredir=sm

47. CDC. *Intimate Partner Violence: Risk and Protective Factors for Perpetration.* https://www.cdc.gov/violenceprevention/intimatepartnerviolence/riskprotectivefactors.html

Chapter 6

48. (Bagshaw & Chung 2000). Bagshaw D & Chung D 2000, Women, Men and Domestic Violence, Commonwealth of Australia, Canberra. Retrieved from: https://www.dcp.wa.gov.au/CrisisAndEmergency/FDV/Documents/2015/FactSheet3Perpetratorcharacte

49. National Coalition Against Domestic Violence (NCADV). *Signs of abuse.* Retrieved from https://ncadv.org/signs-of-abuse

50. National Coalition Against Domestic Violence (NCADV). *Dynamics of abuse.* Retrieved from https://ncadv.org/dynamics-of-abuse

51. Cornerstone 2003. Developed by Cornerstone Foundation, June 2003. *Domestic Violence Counseling Training Manual.* Retrieved from http://www.hotpeachpages.net/camerica/belize/DomesticViolenceTrainingManual.pdf

52. Dutton, D. G. 1998. *The Abusive Personality: Violence and Control in Intimate Relationships.* New York: Guilford Press.

53. Walker, Lenore E. 1979. *The Battered Woman.* New York: Harper and Row.

54. WHO. World Health Organization. *Violence against women.* Retrieved from https://www.who.int/news-room/fact-sheets/detail/violence-against-women

55. Heise, 1998; O'Neil & Harway, 1997. The Factors Influencing Community Attitudes in Relation to Violence Against Women *6.2. Attitudes and the Perpetration of Violence Against Women.* Retrieved from: https://www.vichealth.vic.gov.au/~/media/ProgramsandProjects/DiscriminationandViolence/ViolenceA:

56. Adapted from ECPAT-USA. *Grooming: Is R. Kelly using the same tactics as human traffickers to control his victims?* March 2019. Retrieved from https://www.ecpatusa.org/blog/2019/3/11/grooming-is-r-kelly-using-the-same-tactics-as-human-traffickers-to-control-his-victims

57. DomesticShelters.org, retrieved from https://www.domesticshelters.org/articles/identifying-abuse/from-romance-to-isolation-understanding-grooming

58. Hennessey D. (2004) Presentation in Toledo by Clinical Director of the National Domestic Violence Intervention Agency retrieved and adapted from *Health Service Executive (Ireland) Practice Guide on Domestic, Sexual and Gender Based Violence.* Page 42–43. Retrieved from: https://www.tusla.ie/uploads/content/Domestic_Practice_Guide_on_DSG_bassed_violence.pdf

59. Litton, L. 2007. "Helping St. Louis County Families: A Guide for Court Professionals on the Co-Occurrence of Domestic Violence and Child Abuse/Neglect." Grant No. 2004-WE-AX-K103 awarded by the Office on Violence against Women; Office of Justice Programs, U.S. Department of Justice, supports this project. Lauren J. Litton, I.S.P. Consulting, for the St. Louis County Greenbook Initiative.

60. Adapted from a study by Bonomi, Gangamma, Locke, Katafiasz & Martin, 2011. Source: Andrea B. Jennings, B.S.W., LSW. "Domestic Assault by Strangulation and Recantation of Victims in the Criminal Court System." Retrieved from: https://sophia.stkate.edu/cgi/viewcontent.cgi?

article=1605&context=msw_papers

61. 2013. Government of Western Australia. Dept of Child Protection. *Perpetrator Accountability in Child Protection Practice.* Retrieved from: https://www.dcp.wa.gov.au/CrisisAndEmergency/FDV/Documents/Perpetrator%20Accountability%20i

62. Ibid

63. Alabama Coalition against Domestic Violence. "10 Lies Abusers Frequently Tell." Retrieved from http://acadv.org/warning-signs/are-you-being-abused/

64. Gaslight. English Oxford Living Dictionary. Verb. Retrieved from: https://en.oxforddictionaries.com/definition/gaslight

65. Kashmira Gander. Independent Newspaper UK. October 2018. *Gaslighting. What is it and how can it change a victim's perspective of reality?* Horley, Sandra CBE, chief executive of Refuge. Retrieved from: https://www.independent.co.uk/life-style/health-and-families/gaslighting-and-how-can-it-change-a-victims-perception-of-reality-domestic-abuse-violence-a8575206.html

66. Ibid.

67. Dorpat, Theo. L. (1994). "On the double whammy and gaslighting." Psychoanalysis & Psychotherapy. 11 (1): 91–96. INIST:4017777.

68. Abramson, Kate (2014). "Turning up the Lights on Gaslighting." Philosophical Perspectives. 28 (1): 1–30. doi:10.1111/phpe.12046. ISSN 1520-8583

69. Dorpat, Theodore (2007). Crimes of Punishment: America's Culture of Violence. Algora Publishing. pp. 118–30

70. Evans, Patricia (1996). *The Verbally Abusive Relationship: How to Recognize it and How to Respond* (2nd ed.). Holbrook, Mass.: Adams Media Corporation

71. Greenberg, Elinor. "Are You Being 'Gaslighted' By the Narcissist in Your Life?" Psychology Today. Sussex Publisher. Retrieved 3 April 2018]

72. Kashmira Gander. Independent Newspaper UK. October 2018. Gaslighting. *What is it and how can it change a victim's perspective of reality?* Horley, Sandra CBE, chief executive of Refuge. Retrieved from: https://www.independent.co.uk/life-style/health-and-families/gaslighting-and-how-can-it-change-a-victims-perception-of-reality-domestic-abuse-violence-a8575206.html

73. Bancroft, L. *Why Does He Do That?* Berkley Books 2002

74. Independent Living Resource Centre Thunder Bay http://www.ilrctbay.com/upload/custom/abuse/content/abusers.htm

75. New Hope for Women: *Abuser tricks.* http://www.newhopeforwomen.org/abuser-tricks

76. WebMD: Domestic Abuse: Recognizing the Potential Abuser. Retrieved from: https://www.webmd.com/women/features/domestic-abuse-recognizing -potential-abuser#1

77. Ganley, Anne L. Ph.D. 1998. "Improving the Health Care Response to Domestic Violence: A Trainer's Manual for Health Care Providers." The Family Violence Prevention Fund, Conrad N. Hilton Foundation, and U.S. Department of Health & Human Services. Available at: https://www.futureswithoutviolence.org/userfiles/file/HealthCare/improving_healthcare_healthtrainer.pc

78. Ibid

79. Superior Court of California, County of Fresno. 2013. "Domestic Violence Issues." Retrieved from www.fresno.courts.ca.gov/family/domestic_violence_issues.php

80. State University of New York. Fashion Institute of Technology (FIT). n.d. "Domestic Abuse.' Retrieved from https://www.fitnyc.edu/safety/abuse-stalking-sexual-violence/domestic-abuse.php

81. Litton, L. 2007. "Helping St. Louis County Families: A Guide for Court Professionals on the Co-Occurrence of Domestic Violence and Child Abuse/Neglect." Grant No. 2004-WE-AX-K103 awarded

by the Office on Violence against Women; Office of Justice Programs, U.S. Department of Justice, supports this project. Lauren J. Litton, I.S.P. Consulting, for the St. Louis County Greenbook Initiative.

82. (Norlander & Eckhardt 2005). Source: Department for Child Protection (2013). *Perpetrator Accountability in Child Protection Practice: A resource for child protection workers about engaging and responding to perpetrators of family and domestic violence*, Perth Western Australia: Western Australian Government. Page 14: Failure to manage emotions (such as anger or stress). Retrieved from https://www.dcp.wa.gov.au/CrisisAndEmergency/FDV/Documents/Perpetrator%20Accountability%20i

83. North Carolina Domestic Violence Commission. N.C. Abuser Treatment Committee and the N.C. Council for Women. 'Batterer Intervention Programs. A Guide to Achieving Recommended Practices.' Why not anger management? Pages 9-11. Retrieved from https://files.nc.gov/ncdoa/documents/files/BattererInterventionHandbook.pdf

84. Adapted from The National Domestic Violence Hotline: *Why We Don't Recommend Couples Counseling for Abusive Relationships*. Retrieved from: https://www.thehotline.org/2014/08/01/why-we-dont-recommend-couples-counseling-for-abusive-relationships/

85. Department of Children and Families Florida. 'Batterers Intervention Programs.' https://www.myflfamilies.com/service-programs/domestic-violence/batterer-intervention-program.shtml

86. Government of Australia. *Perpetrator Accountability in Child Protection Practice*. Retrieved from: https://www.dcp.wa.gov.au/CrisisAnd Emergency/FDV/Documents/Perpetrator%20Accountability%20in%20Child%20Protection%20Practice

87. Clark County Prosecuting Attorney's Office. 2012. Myths and Facts about Domestic Violence. Retrieved from www.clarkprosecutor.org/html/domviol/myths.htm

Chapter 7

88. Walker, Lenore E. 1979. *The Battered Woman*. New York: Harper and Row.

89. Ibid

90. Adapted from the National Domestic Abuse Hotline's 'Is Abuse Really a 'Cycle'?' Retrieved from https://www.thehotline.org/2013/08/15/is-abuse-really-a-cycle/

91. The Cycle of Violence (adapted). Walker 1979.

92. The Deluth Model of Power and Control. Retrieved from https://www.theduluthmodel.org/wheels/understanding-power-control-wheel/

93. The National Domestic Violence Hotline. LGBTQ+ power and control wheel. http://www.thehotline.org/wp-content/uploads/sites/3/2015/01/LGBT-Wheel.pdf

Chapter 8

94. Itzin C, Taket A, Barter-Godfrey S. Domestic and sexual violence and abuse. London, New York: Routledge; 2010

95. World Health Organization. *Violence against women*. Retrieved from https://www.who.int/news-room/fact-sheets/detail/violence-against-women

96. Taylor N.T. Brown and Jody L. Herman. 2015. The Williams Institute, UCLA School of Law. *Intimate partner violence and sexual abuse among LGBT people–a review of research*. Available at: https://williamsinstitute.law.ucla.edu/wp-content/uploads/Intimate-Partner-Violence-and-Sexual-Abuse-among-LGBT-People.pdf

97. Adapted from Healthtalk.org: *Women's experiences of Domestic Violence and Abuse*. Retrieved from http://www.healthtalk.org/peoples-experiences/domestic-violence-abuse/womens-experiences-domestic-violence-and-abuse/impact-domestic-violence-and-abuse-womens-mental-health

98. Geanacopoulos, P. 1999. *Domestic Violence: A training manual for the Greek Orthodox Community,* " Page 11. Retrieved from https://www.scribd.com/document/259090061/DOMESTIC-VIOLENCE-A-Training-Manual-for-the-Greek-Orthodox-Community

99. Amanda Kippert. 2017. Domesticshelters.org. 'Why We Blame Victims for Domestic Violence.' Retrieved from https://www.domesticshelters.org/articles/domestic-violence/why-so-many-are-quick-to-blame-victims-of-domestic-violence

100. Adapted from Sarah M. Buel's *50 Obstacles to Leaving, a.k.a. Why Abuse Victims Stay.* The National Domestic Abuse Hotline. Retrieved from: https://www.thehotline.org/is-this-abuse/why-do-people-stay-in-abusive-relationships

100a. Adapted from: *The Domestic Violence Hotline: Domestic Violence & People with Disabilities.* https://www.thehotline.org/is-this-abuse/domestic-violence-disabilities-2/

100b. Center for Disease Control (CDC). National Center for Injury Prevention and Control. *Understanding elder abuse.* https://www.cdc.gov/violenceprevention/pdf/em-factsheet-a.pdf

Chapter 9

101. National Society For the Prevention of Abuse to Children (NSPCC). 'Domestic abuse. What is domestic abuse?' Retrieved from: https://www.nspcc.org.uk/preventing-abuse/child-abuse-and-neglect/domestic-abuse/

102. Harris-Johnson C 2005, *Come with Daddy: Child murder-suicide after family breakdown,* University of Western Australia Press, Perth.

103. Humphreys C 2007, 'Family and domestic violence and child protection: Challenging directions for practice', *Issues Paper 13,* University of New South Wales, Sydney.

104. Edleson J 1999, 'The overlap between child maltreatment and woman battering', *Violence Against Women,* 5: 134–154.

104a. Daly, E. 2014. *Child abuse: What you need to know.* Parker Publishing/Amazon

105. Frieze, I. H. and Browne, A. 1989. "Violence in Marriage." In L. E. Ohlin and M. H. Tonry, *Family Violence.* Chicago, IL: University of Chicago Press. Break the Cycle. 2006. "Startling Statistics." In Speak Up. Speak Out. Speak Now!

106. Daly, E. 2014. *Child abuse: What you need to know.* Parker Publishing/Amazon.

107. Government of Australia. *Perpetrator Accountability in Child Protection Practice.* Retrieved from: https://www.dcp.wa.gov.au/CrisisAndEmergency/FDV/Documents/Perpetrator%20Accountability%20in%20Child%20Protection%20Practice

108. Ehrensaft, M. K., Cohen, P., Brown, J., Smailes, E., Chen, H., and Johnson, J. G. 2003. "Intergenerational Transmission of Partner Violence: A 20-Year Prospective Study." Journal of Consulting & Clinical Psychology 71:741–753.

109. Shonokoff, J. P. and Phillips, D. A., 2000. From Neurons to Neighborhoods: The Science of Early Childhood Development. Washington, DC: National Academies Press.

110. Chicago Foundation for Women. 2007. What Will It Take? Campaign. "Types of Violence."

111. Adapted from the National Child Traumatic Stress Network, Domestic Violence Collaborative Group. (2010). Domestic violence and children: Questions and answers for domestic violence project advocates. Retrieved from http://www.doj.state.or.us/wp-content/uploads/2017/08/domestic_violence_and_children.pdf

112. Ibid

113. National Society For the Prevention of Abuse to Children (NSPCC). 'Domestic abuse. What is domestic abuse?' Retrieved from: https://www.nspcc.org.uk/preventing-abuse/child-abuse-and-

neglect/domestic-abuse/

114. Litton, L. 2007. "Helping St. Louis County Families: A Guide for Court Professionals on the Co-Occurrence of Domestic Violence and Child Abuse/Neglect." Grant No. 2004-WE-AX-K103 awarded by the Office on Violence against Women; Office of Justice Programs, U.S. Department of Justice, supports this project. Lauren J. Litton, I.S.P. Consulting, for the St. Louis County Greenbook Initiative.

115. Daly, E. 2014. *Child abuse: What you need to know.* Parker Publishing/Amazon.

116. Adapted from Litton, L. 2007. "Helping St. Louis County Families: A Guide for Court Professionals on the Co-Occurrence of Domestic Violence and Child Abuse/Neglect." Grant No. 2004-WE-AX-K103 awarded by the Office on Violence against Women; Office of Justice Programs, U.S. Department of Justice, supports this project. Lauren J. Litton, I.S.P. Consulting, for the St. Louis County Greenbook Initiative.

117. *When Children Witness Domestic Violence.* Alayne Yates MD, Professor and Director, Division of Child and Adolescent Psychiatry, University of Hawaii, 1996

118. Litton 2007/ National Society for the Prevention of Cruelty to Children. (NSPCC) *Domestic abuse. Signs, indicators and effects.* Retrieved from https://www.nspcc.org.uk/preventing-abuse/child-abuse-and-neglect/domestic-abuse/signs-symptoms-effects

119. Department of Justice: The National Child Traumatic Stress Network: Domestic Violence and Children Questions and Answers for Domestic Violence Project Advocates. Retrieved from http://www.doj.state.or.us/wp-content/uploads/2017/08/domestic_violence_and_children.pdf

Chapter 10

120. White, D. (2013). Psych Central. 'Recognizing the Signs of Domestic Violence.' Retrieved from http://psychcentral.com/blog/archives/2013/09/28/recognizing-the-signs-of-domestic-violence/

121. Helpguide.org. 2016. "Domestic Violence and Abuse: Signs of Abuse and Abusive Relationships." Authors: Melinda Smith, M.A., and Jeanne Segal, Ph.D. Retrieved from http://www.helpguide.org/articles/abuse/domestic-violence-and-abuse.htm

121a. Campbell JC, Webster D, Koziol-McLain J, Block C, Campbell D, Curry MA, et al. Risk Factors for Femicide in Abusive Relationships: Results from a Multisite Case Control Study. American Journal of Public Health, 2003, 93(7):1089–1097. World Health Organization. *Intimate partner violence during pregnancy*
https://apps.who.int/iris/bitstream/handle/10665/70764/WHO_RHR_11.35_eng.pdf;jsessionid=194C65!sequence=1

122. Gazmararian JA, Lazorick S, Spitz AM et al. 1996. Prevalence of violence against pregnant women. JAMA 275: 1915-20.

123. New York City Mayor's Office to Combat Domestic Violence. "Medical Providers' Guide to Managing the Care of Domestic Violence Patients Within a Cultural Context," Retrieved from http://www.nyc.gov/html/ocdv/downloads/pdf/Materials_Medical_Providers_DV_Guide.pdf

124. American Medical Association Diagnostic and Treatment Guidelines on Domestic Violence. https://www.nlm.nih.gov/exhibition/confronting violence/materials/OB11102.pdf

125. "Doctors vs Domestic Violence: Yes, you can make a difference," Gail Garfinkel Weiss. https://www.medicaleconomics.com/clinical-pharmacology/doctors-vs-domestic-violence-yes-you-can-make-difference

Chapter 11

126. Geanacopoulos, P. 1999. *Domestic Violence: A training manual for the Greek Orthodox Community,* Page 7. Retrieved from https://www.scribd.com/document/259090061/DOMESTIC-VIOLENCE-A-Training-Manual-for-the-Greek-Orthodox-Community

127. Kasperkevic, Jana. (Guardian) *Up to 75% of abused women who are murdered are killed after they leave their partners.* https://www.theguardian.com/money/us-money-blog/2014/oct/20/domestic-private-violence-women-men-abuse-hbo-ray-rice

128. The National Domestic Violence Hotline – adapted from Sarah M. Buel's "50 Obstacles to Leaving, a.k.a Why Abuse Victims Stay." Retrieved from: https://www.thehotline.org/is-this-abuse/why-do-people-stay-in-abusive-relationships

129. Anne Ganley, PhD, and Margaret Hobart, PhD 2016. Washington State Department of Social and Health Services. 'A social worker's guide to domestic violence.' Available from https://wscadv.org/wp-content/uploads/2019/01/DCYF-DV-Guide.pdf

130. Adapted from The Domestic Violence Hotline: Safety Planning with Children. Retrieved from: https://www.thehotline.org/2013/04/12/safety-planning-with-children

131. Litton, L. 2007. "Helping St. Louis County Families: A Guide for Court Professionals on the Co-Occurrence of Domestic Violence and Child Abuse/Neglect." Page 12. Grant No. 2004-WE-AX-K103 awarded by the Office on Violence against Women; Office of Justice Programs, U.S. Department of Justice, supports this project. Lauren J. Litton, I.S.P. Consulting, for the St. Louis County Greenbook Initiative.

132. Ibid

133. Jaffe, P., Crooks, C., and Wong, F. Q. F. 2005. *Journal of the Center for families, Children and the Courts.* "Parenting Arrangements After Domestic Violence." Retrieved from: https://www.researchgate.net/publication/237393224_Parenting_Arrangements_After_Domestic_Violer

134. Also see: https://www.childwelfare.gov/topics/systemwide/dom_violence/collaboration/courts/

135. Daly, E. 2014. *Child abuse: What you need to know.* Parker Publishing/Amazon

136. Daly. E, Wright, John, MD, FAAP. 2017. *Child abuse. Prevention through understanding.* Parker Publishing/Amazon.

137. DayOne Services. 'Going to a shelter.' https://dayoneservices.org/going-to-a-shelter/

Chapter 12

138. Litton, L. 2007. "Helping St. Louis County Families: A Guide for Court Professionals on the Co-Occurrence of Domestic Violence and Child Abuse/Neglect." Grant No. 2004-WE-AX-K103 awarded by the Office on Violence against Women; Office of Justice Programs, U.S. Department of Justice, supports this project. Lauren J. Litton, I.S.P. Consulting, for the St. Louis County Greenbook Initiative.

138a. Female Domestic Violence Victims: Perspectives on Emergency Care. Betty Wendt Mayer, RN; MSN College of Nursing, University of South Florida, Tampa. http://citeseerx.ist.psu.edu/viewdoc/download?doi=10.1.1.854.4419&rep=rep1&type=pdf

College of Family Physicians of Canada. Canadian Family Physician 1999. Domestic violence is the leading cause of injury to women aged 15 to 44. https://www.ncbi.nlm.nih.gov/pmc/articles/PMC2328613/pdf/canfamphys00044-0059.pdf

139. *Washington Post.* How domestic violence leads to murder. Domestic slayings: Brutal and foreseeable. https://www.washingtonpost.com/graphics/2018/investigations/domestic-violence-murders/?utm_term=.4a439ade8ed1

139a. CDC: Half of All Female Homicide Victims Are Killed by Intimate Partners. https://www.npr.org/sections/thetwo-way/2017/07/21/538518569/cdc-half-of-all-female-murder-victims-are-killed-by-intimate-partners

140. The Human Rights Campaign. Retrieved from https://www.hrc.org/blog/common-myths-about-LGBTQ$^+$-domestic-violence

141. U.S. National Library of Medicine 2011. Kevin L. Ard, MD and Harvey J. Makadon MD.

"Addressing Intimate Partner Violence in Lesbian, Gay, Bisexual, and Transgender Patients." Retrieved from: https://www.ncbi.nlm.nih.gov/pmc/articles/PMC3138983/

142. The National Intimate Partner and Sexual Violence Survey. 2010 Findings on Victimization by Sexual Orientation. Retrieved from: https://www.cdc.gov/violenceprevention/pdf/nisvs_sofindings.pdf

143. Office of Justice Programs. Journal of Family Violence Volume:24. Issue: 2 February 2009. Pages 87–93. Perceptions of Same-Sex Domestic Violence Among Crisis Center Staff. Michael J. Brown; Jennifer Groscup. Retrieved from: https://www.ncjrs.gov/App/Publications/abstract.aspx?ID=248000

144. Taylor N.T. Brown and Jody L. Herman. 2015. The Williams Institute, UCLA School of Law. Intimate partner violence and sexual abuse among LGBT people–a review of research. Available at: https://williamsinstitute.law.ucla.edu/wp-content/uploads/Intimate-Partner-Violence-and-Sexual-Abuse-among-LGBT-People.pdf

145. Ibid.

146. The National Intimate Partner and Sexual Violence Survey. 2010 Findings on Victimization by Sexual Orientation. Retrieved from: https://www.cdc.gov/violenceprevention/pdf/nisvs_sofindings.pdf

147. Ibid.

148. U.S. National Library of Medicine 2011. Kevin L. Ard, MD and Harvey J. Makadon MD. "Addressing Intimate Partner Violence in Lesbian, Gay, Bisexual, and Transgender Patients." Retrieved from: https://www.ncbi.nlm.nih.gov/pmc/articles/PMC3138983/

149. UC Hastings. College of the Law San Francisco. "Perceiving and Reporting Domestic Violence Incidents in Unconventional Settings: A Vignette Survey Study." Retrieved from: https://repository.uchastings.edu/faculty_scholarship/9/

150. Office of Justice Programs. Journal of Family Violence Volume:24. Issue:2 February 2009. Pages:87-93. "Perceptions of Same-Sex Domestic Violence Among Crisis Center Staff." Michael J. Brown; Jennifer Groscup. Retrieved from: https://www.ncjrs.gov/App/Publications/abstract.aspx?ID=248000

151. Business Insider. Dodgson, Lindsay. 2017. "People often stay in abusive relationships because of something called 'trauma bonding'—here are the signs it's happening to you."

Chapter 13

152. US Department of Justice. 1117, Restrictions on the possession of firearms by individuals convicted of a misdemeanor crime of domestic violence. https://www.justice.gov/jm/criminal-resource-manual-1117-restrictions-possession-firearms-individuals-convicted

153. Federal Bureau of Investigation, Federal Denials, November 30, 1998 –April 30, 2018, https://www.fbi.gov/file-repository/federal_denials.pdf/view]

154. Adapted from FindLaw. 'Domestic Violence Restraining Order FAQs.' Retrieved from https://family.findlaw.com/domestic-violence/domestic-violence-restraining-order-faqs.html

National Network to End Domestic Violence. Womenslaw.org. https://www.womenslaw.org/laws/fl/restraining-orders/injunctions-protection-against-domestic-violence/basic-info

155. Fetters, Ashley. July 2018. The Atlantic. *Why It's Hard to Protect Domestic-Violence Survivors Online.* https://www.theatlantic.com/family/archive/2018/07/restraining-orders-social-media/564614/

Chapter 14

156. Daly, Martin, and Margo Wilson, M. 2005. "The 'Cinderella Effect': Elevated Mistreatment of Stepchildren in Comparison to Those Living with Genetic Parents." *Trends in Cognitive Sciences* 9:507

156a. Dutton, D. G. and Painter, S. L. 1981. "Traumatic Bonding: The Development of Emotional Attachments in Battered Women and Other Relationships of Intermittent Abuse." Victimology: An

International Journal 6(1–4):139–155.

Chapter 15

157. Huffington Post, Crime. *Domestic Violence Murders Are Suddenly on the Rise.* Melissa Jeltsen. April 11, 2019.
https://www.huffpost.com/entry/domestic-violence-murders-rising_n_5cae0d92e4b03ab9f24f2e6d

158. World Health Organization. 2017. 'Violence against women.' https://www.who.int/en/news-room/fact-sheets/detail/violence-against-women

159. National Crime Victimization Survey (NCVS). U.S. Department of Justice: Nonfatal Domestic Violence, 2003–2012. Retrieved from: https://www.bjs.gov/content/pub/pdf/ndv0312.pdf

160. Committee on the Judiciary, U.S. Senate, 102nd Congress. 1992 (October). "Violence Against Women: A Majority Staff Report," p. 3.

161. National Crime Victimization Survey (NCVS). U.S. Department of Justice: Nonfatal Domestic Violence, 2003–2012 https://www.bjs.gov/content/pub/pdf/ndv0312.pdf

162. Bureau of Justice. 1995. National Crime Victimization Survey https://www.bjs.gov/content/pub/pdf/FEMVIED.PDF

163. National Center for Biotechnology Information: Canadian Family Physician Retrieved from https://www.ncbi.nlm.nih.gov/pmc/articles/PMC2328613/pdf/canfamphys00044-0059.pdf

164. National Center for Biotechnology Information: Canadian Family Physician Retrieved from https://www.ncbi.nlm.nih.gov/pmc/articles/PMC2328613/pdf/canfamphys00044-0059.pdf

165. Centers for Disease Control (CDC): *Prevalence and Characteristics of Sexual Violence, Stalking, and Intimate Partner Violence Victimization—National Intimate Partner and Sexual Violence Survey, United States, 2011.* Retrieved from https://www.cdc.gov/mmwr/preview/mmwrhtml/ss6308a1.htm

166. Campbell, J. C., et al. 2003. "Assessing Risk Factors for Intimate Partner Homicide." *NIJ Journal 250* (November), NCJ 196547. Also See: NYS Office for the Prevention of Domestic Violence. Retrieved from https://www.ncjrs.gov/pdffiles1/jr000250e.pdf

167. *American Journal of Public Health.* July 2003. Risk Factors for Femicide in busive Relationships: Results From a Multisite Case Control Study. Retrieved from: https://www.ncbi.nlm.nih.gov/pmc/articles/PMC1447915/

168. Violence Policy Center. (2013, April). Firearm Justifiable Homicides and Non-Fatal Self-Defense Gun Use: An Analysis of Federal Bureau of Investigation and National Crime Victimization Survey Data. Washington, DC. Retrieved from: https://nrcdv.org/dvam/sites/default/files2/FirearmsandDV-TalkingPointsForm.pdf

169. US Department of Justice. *Nonfatal Domestic Violence, 2003–2012.* April 2014. Retrieved from https://www.bjs.gov/content/pub/pdf/ndv0312.pdf

170. "Black, American Indian and Alaska Native women are murdered at a rate nearly 2.5 times higher than white women." Center for Disease Control (CDC). 2017. Retrieved from https://www.news5cleveland.com/news/local-news/investigations/cdc-black-women-experience-highest-rates-of-homicide-of-any-racial-group-in-the-united-states

171. Campbell, J. C., et al. 2003. "Assessing Risk Factors for Intimate Partner Homicide." *NIJ Journal 250* (November), NCJ 196547. Also See: NYS Office for the Prevention of Domestic Violence. Retrieved from https://www.ncjrs.gov/pdffiles1/jr000250e.pdf

172. Sharps, P., Campbell, J. C., Campbell, D. Gary, F., and Webster, D. 2003. "Risky Mix: Drinking, Drug Use, and Homicide." *NIJ Journal 250.* Retrieved from https://www.ncjrs.gov/pdffiles1/jr000250d.pdf

173. Sorenson, Susan B. (professor of social policy in the University of Pennsylvania School of Social Policy & Practice) 'Dating partners commit more domestic abuse than spouses.' Retrieved from: https://www.futurity.org/dating-partners-violence-1668592-2/

174. Catalano, S. 2012. "Intimate Partner Violence, 1993–2010." Page 4. U.S. Department of Justice, Special Report. Retrieved from http://bjs.ojp.usdoj.gov/content/pub/pdf/ipv9310.pdf

Bureau of Justice Statistics (BJS). Nonfatal Domestic Violence, 2003–2012. Retrieved from:

175. National Coalition Against Domestic Violence (NCADV) https://ncadv.org/blog/posts/domestic-violence-and-people-with-disabilities

176. National Council on Aging https://www.ncoa.org/public-policy-action/elder-justice/elder-abuse-facts/

177. National Coalition Against Domestic Violence (NCADV) https://ncadv.org/blog/posts/domestic-violence-and-the-LGBTQ±-community

Printed in Great Britain
by Amazon